Three American Romantic Painters

Charles Burchfield
with an introduction by Alfred H. Barr, Jr.

Florine Stettheimer
by Henry McBride

Franklin C. Watkins
by Andrew Carnduff Ritchie

The Museum of Modern Art, New York
Reprint Edition, 1969
Published for The Museum of Modern Art by Arno Press

ND
236
T442
1969

CHARLES BURCHFIELD
EARLY WATERCOLORS

APRIL 11   1930   APRIL 26

MUSEUM OF MODERN ART

730 FIFTH AVENUE   NEW YORK

ACKNOWLEDGMENT

The exhibition has been selected from the following collections:

In addition to those who have lent pictures the Trustees and the Staff wish to thank Mr. Frank K. M. Rehn, the artist's representative, for his assistance in assembling the exhibition.

TRUSTEES

INTRODUCTION

To those who are familiar with Charles Burchfield's mature style his early work now exhibited for the first time must appear surprising and even contradictory.

In his recent work which has placed him among the most interesting American artists Burchfield has examined critically the mid-western town: its houses, its railroad yards and eating places, its false fronted stores, Garfield Gothic churches, and telegraph poles confronting their reflections in main street puddles. Satire in which hate and wit are mingled is combined with the discovery of picturesque ugliness. In these gray, silver and black watercolors that authentically native movement which might be christened American-Scenism is seen at its pictorial best.

In his earlier work we find an astonishingly different spirit. Frequently the same objects appear—small town, post-Civil War buildings—but they are not so much satirized as eagerly accepted as material for romantic composition. A more essential similarity between his familiar later work and these early inventions lies in the very fact that in both Burchfield was thoroughly interested in subject matter at a time when interest in subject matter was generally discredited.

During this early Romantic Period Burchfield concentrated upon the expression of moods and emotions on the one hand, and on the other upon specific forces and even sounds and movements of nature. His method was neither vague nor spontaneous as is frequent in expressionistic painting, but deliberate and precise. Of the "Night Wind" (No. 26) Burchfield writes: "To the child sitting cozily in his home the roar of the wind outside fills his mind full of strange visions and phantoms flying over the land." In the painting the patterns which surround the house are of two kinds—the torn black silhouette suggests the terrific force of the wind blowing from left to right, while the white wave beyond tosses monstrous half-organic arms which threaten to overwhelm the child's home. These two abstract motives of force and fear were studied and re-studied in a long series of drawings before they reached completion in the finished picture. Similar and equally successful is the uncanny "Church Bells Ringing" (No. 17). In the sky are the same menacing waves. The church tower assumes a face like an African mask and sways with the swinging spiral motion and sound of the bells. Spiral and wave inflect the eaves and windows of the house. The whole scene rocks and quails before the horrid clangour. Again invisible sound and the resulting emotion are realized in visual forms.

More elegiac in mood is the "Garden of Memories" (No. 25) in which an aged woman sits in the tired moonlight while colossal lunar flowers surge and droop about her. The "August North" (No. 14) is similar in mood but more direct in statement. In striking contrast is the "Song of the Katydids" (No. 18) in which the vibrations of heat, the monotonous vibrations of insects, are diagrammed. Houses and trees quiver beneath the hot feet of summer's noon.

Many of the watercolors are less dependent upon expressionistic devices. The haunted gloom of the swamp pervades "First Hepaticas" (No. 27) and the "Fallen Tree" (No. 9). In the "Rogues' Gallery" (No. 4) and "The Conference" (No. 10) we find a delightful feeling for the grotesquely humorous. "Summer Rain" (No. 1) and "Hot Morning Sunlight" (No. 7) which come early in the series are frankly decorative, more purely aesthetic in their interest.

It is impossible to discover any important external influence upon Burchfield's art. These watercolors were painted in Salem, Ohio, between 1916 and the early months of 1918. In the previous four years he had attended the Cleveland Art School where Henry G. Keller had encouraged him to use his imagination rather than to follow the conventional Impressionist methods of the period. He was almost completely ignorant of what had happened in Europe. He does not remember having seen a Cézanne before 1920. He saw his first van Gogh in 1929. He believes that Japanese prints may have had some influence upon his design but cannot remember any conscious admiration for Oriental art before 1918. One can only conclude that we have in this period of Burchfield's development one of the most isolated and original phenomena in American Art.

Several analogies of course suggest themselves. The patterns of "Night Wind" (No. 26) remind one of van Gogh's cloud structures. The vibrations which radiate from the sun in "Cat-tails" (No. 3) and from the trees in "Song of the Katydids" (No. 18) also suggest van Gogh's drawings as does the muscular activity of the "Beech Trees" (No. 21). But Burchfield's invention of abstract motives as direct visual symbols for invisible forces bring him close to the technical methods of Chinese and Japanese painting in which clouds, waves, and flames are transformed into linear formulae. It is but a short step psychologically from the wind monster with its saucer eyes (No. 26) to the more highly developed Dragon of water and air which appears half submerged in the torrential waterfalls of the Sung painters.

In several instances our closest analogies are to be found in German and English romantic art of the early 19th century. Samuel Palmer might have admired the "Garden of Memories"; Caspar David Friedrich the "First Hepaticas." In Burchfield's art the "Gothick" moods of melancholy and terror are re-born a century later. And curiously enough in such pictures as "Wheat field with Tower" (No. 11), "Church Bells Ringing" (No. 17) and most strikingly in

"Sunday Morning" (No. 12) one feels the influence of the silhouettes, the textures, the Spencerian flourishes, the very wall-papers and stained glass of the mid-19th century, assimilated (but not consciously admired as they were to be twelve years later in 1930).

Very curious too is Burchfield's attempt in his early twenties to re-create the sensations and emotions of his childhood: "The child stands alone in the garden—(No. 15)"; "The church bell is ringing and it terrifies me (the child)—(No. 17)"; "The child sits listening—(No. 13)." Much of 1917 was devoted to this problem.

The surrender to mood, the attempt to present sound and energy in terms of vision, the love of the "rustic," the "picturesque," the "melancholy" and the "terrible," the nostalgia for childhood, the use of "literary" titles, are all romantic qualities or vices—but there is also in Burchfield's art discipline, strength of design and a clarity of purpose which raises these youthful watercolors to a high level of original achievement even as formal inventions.

CHRONOLOGY

1893   Born at Ashtabula Harbor, Ohio, April 9th.

1898   Moved to Salem, Ohio, where he lived until 1921.

1911–16 Studied at the Cleveland School of Art. Encouraged by Henry G. Keller. Worked during summers and until 1921 as costs accountant in automobile parts company.

1920   First exhibition in New York made possible by Mrs. Mary Mowbray-Clarke. Has since exhibited in many American cities and in London (1923) and Paris (1925).

1921–28 Worked as designer of wallpapers in Buffalo.
           Now lives in Gardenville, New York.

1929   Winter. Work of the Romantic Period (1916–18) re-discovered by Edward W. Root.

Other watercolors are in the following collections:

BROOKLYN, MUSEUM OF ART

BUFFALO, ALBRIGHT ART GALLERY

CLEVELAND, MUSEUM OF ART

NEWARK, ART MUSEUM

NEW YORK, METROPOLITAN MUSEUM OF ART

NEW YORK, MUSEUM OF MODERN ART

NEW YORK, WHITNEY MUSEUM

PHILADELPHIA, PENNSYLVANIA ACADEMY OF THE FINE ARTS

WASHINGTON, PHILLIPS MEMORIAL GALLERY

CATALOG

Notes on the pictures are by Mr. Burchfield

1 SUMMER RAIN
19⅞ x 13⅞ inches
Signed and dated lower right, Sept. 1916
Private Collection, New York

Raindrops like jewels hang on sunflower plants.

2 THE CITY
14 x 19¾ inches
Signed and dated lower right, 1916

Layer after layer of sections of the city extending out to the horizon like long rolling ocean waves, cut by the brilliant reflections of sun on polished slate roofs.

3 CAT-TAILS
14 x 19⅞ inches
Signed and dated lower left, 1916   ILLUSTRATED

Cat-tails growing in front of a pile of mine refuse, the March sun shining—lacy trees.
Painted while home from school on a spring vacation.

4 ROGUES' GALLERY
13⅞ x 19¾ inches
Signed and dated lower right, 1916   ILLUSTRATED

A rogues' gallery of sunflowers in the brilliant, dry sunshine of August.

5 DRIFTING DANDELION SEEDS
14 x 19⅞ inches
Signed and dated lower left, 1916
Collection Thomas Metcalf, Boston

Wingèd dandelion seeds scattered obliquely across the overlapping layers of a hayfield by a fresh June wind.

6 DECORATIVE LANDSCAPE: SHADOW
19¾ x 13⅝ inches
Signed and dated lower right, 1916
Collection Edward W. Root, Clinton, New York

Color notes are recorded on the painting.

7 DECORATIVE LANDSCAPE: HOT MORNING SUNLIGHT
13¾ x 19½ inches
Signed and dated lower right, 1916
Collection Edward W. Root, Clinton, New York

The air is heavy with humidity—the sky covered with a thick mist, on which the sun shines, seeming to turn it into brilliant steam; it is one of those oppressively hot mornings which always end in a violent thunderstorm in the afternoon.

8 PORTRAIT STUDY—IN A DOORWAY
25 x 29⅞ inches
Painted January 1917
Collection Mrs. Alice M. Burchfield, Salem, Ohio   ILLUSTRATED
>Not an attempt to produce a "bona fide" portrait, but merely a study of a mood in which the figure is simply one of many objects.

9 A FALLEN TREE
18 x 21 inches
Signed and dated lower right, Feb. 24, 1917
Private Collection, New York
>A fallen sycamore tree sprawling over a frozen swamp pond with a wild, haunted marsh tangle behind.

10 THE CONFERENCE
14 x 19⅞ inches
Painted March 3, 1917

11 WHEAT FIELD WITH TOWER
22 x 17¾ inches
Signed and dated lower left, June 1917
>The last rays of the sun on a tower in front of a field of young wheat.

12 SUNDAY MORNING AT ELEVEN O'CLOCK (A recollection of a childhood mood)
21¾ x 17¾ inches
Painted June 1917
Collection Frank K. M. Rehn, New York
>I had had a quarrel with my Sunday-school teacher, and had run outside. Wishing to avoid the embarrassment of having to explain at home my premature return from Sunday-school, I hung around in the church-yard until the class was dismissed. A still, hot June morning; the Sunday quiet had settled down over the town—trees stood motionless as if yearning toward the sun; the roses drooped in the heat; all things seemed blended in one harmonious whole; I only was out of harmony.

13 A MEMORY FROM CHILDHOOD
17⅝ x 22 inches
Signed and dated lower right, July 28, 1917
Collection Mrs. Courtlandt D. Barnes, New York
>Long summer noon hours in the woods—the dazzling white sun spreads fantastic shapes over the dark floor under the trees—the child sits listening to the hum of insects, dreaming of fairies.

14 THE AUGUST NORTH (A memory of childhood)
24½ x 18½ inches
Signed and dated lower right, August 1917
>In August at the last fading of twilight the North assumed to the child a fearful aspect (that colored his thoughts even into early manhood). A melancholy settles down over the child's world—he is as if in a tomb—he thinks all his loved ones are gone away or dead—the ghostly white petunias droop with sadness—unnamed terrors lurk in the black caverns under bushes and trees—as the darkness settles down, the pulsating chorus of night insects commences swelling louder and louder until it resembles the heart beat of the interior of a black closet.

15 THE INSECT CHORUS

20 x 15 ⅞ inches

Signed lower right, 1917—Painted September 5

Collection Edward W. Root, Clinton, New York

> It is late Sunday afternoon in August, the child stands alone in the garden listening to the metallic sounds of insects; they are all his world, so to his mind all things become saturated with their presence—crickets lurk in the depths of the grass, the shadows of the trees conceal fantastic creatures, and the boy looks with fear at the black interior of the arbor, not knowing what terrible thing might be there.

16 PORTRAIT OF MY AUNT EMILY

27 ⅜ x 18 inches

Painted September 22–26, 1917

Collection Mrs. Alice M. Burchfield, Salem, Ohio

> Aunt Em's home always fascinated me as a boy—the old grandfather clock with its slow, stately ticking—the naïve portrait of a black cat—the picture of old-fashioned flowers—the rag carpets, etc.

17 CHURCH BELLS RINGING—RAINY WINTER NIGHT

30 x 19 inches

Signed and dated lower right, December 1917

Collection Miss Louise M. Dunn, Cleveland   ILLUSTRATED

> From a letter dated March 5, 1929: "It was an attempt to express a childhood emotion—a rainy winter night—the churchbell is ringing and it terrifies me (the child)—the bell ringing motive reaches out and saturates the rainy sky—the roofs of the houses dripping with rain are influenced; the child attempts to be comforted by the thoughts of candle lights and Christmas trees, but the fear of the black, rainy night is overpowering. When I think back on such things I know what R——— means by the 'pang in the middle of the night'."

18 THE SONG OF THE KATYDIDS ON AN AUGUST MORNING

17 ¾ x 21 ¾ inches

Signed and dated lower right, 1917

Collection Frank K. M. Rehn, New York   ILLUSTRATED

> A stagnant August morning during the drought season; as the pitiless sun mounts into the mid-morning sky the insect chorus commences, the katydids and locusts predominating; their monotonous, mechanical, brassy rhythms soon pervade the whole air, combining with heat waves of the sun, and saturating trees and houses and sky.

19 CHILDHOOD'S GARDEN

27 x 18 ⅞ inches

Signed and dated lower right, 1917

Collection Edward W. Root, Clinton, New York

> A memory of childhood—an attempt to re-create the way a flower garden looks to a child.

20 THE WINDOW BY THE ALLEY

18 x 22 inches

Painted 1917   ILLUSTRATED

21 BEECH TREES
21¾ x 17¾ inches
Signed and dated lower right, 1917   ILLUSTRATED

22 THE SOUTHEAST SNOWSTORM
17¾ x 19½ inches
Dated lower right, 1917

23 THE BARN
14 x 19⅞ inches
Signed and dated lower right, 1917

24 THE EAST WIND
18 x 22 inches
Painted January 1918

> The East wind brings rain—to the child in his bed, the wind is a fabulous monster and the days of rain on the roof are frightful.

25 GARDEN OF MEMORIES
25¾ x 22½ inches
Signed lower right
Painted August-September 1917
Private Collection, New York   ILLUSTRATED

> Crabbed old age sits in front of her black doorway, without hope for the future, brooding. Spiders lurk in dark corners; the dying plants reflect her mood. The romantic autumn moon rises just the same.

26 THE NIGHT WIND
21¼ x 21¾ inches
Painted January 1918
Private Collection, New York   ILLUSTRATED

> To the child sitting cozily in his home, the roar of the wind outside fills his mind full of visions of strange phantoms and monsters flying over the land.

27 THE FIRST HEPATICAS
22 x 27¾ inches
Painted March 1918   ILLUSTRATED

> It is late March; it has been raining. Walking along through the barren woods in the dusk, I come upon the first hepaticas; the drooping unopened buds, exquisite in their delicateness, present a striking contrast to the black, evil-looking tree trunks.

ILLUSTRATIONS

3
CAT-TAILS, 1916
14 x 19⅞ inches

4
ROGUES' GALLERY, 1916
13 7/8 x 19 3/4 inches

8

PORTRAIT STUDY—IN A DOORWAY, 1917

25 x 29⅞ inches

Collection Mrs. Alice M. Burchfield, Salem, Ohio

CHURCH BELLS RINGING—RAINY WINTER NIGHT, 1917

30 x 19 inches

Collection Miss Louise M. Dunn, Cleveland

18
THE SONG OF THE KATYDIDS ON AN AUGUST MORNING, 1917
17¾ x 21¾ inches
Collection Frank K. M. Rehn, New York

20

THE WINDOW BY THE ALLEY, 1917
18 x 22 inches

21

BEECH TREES, 1917

21¾ x 17¾ inches

25

GARDEN OF MEMORIES, 1917
25¾ x 22½ inches
Private Collection, New York

26
THE NIGHT WIND, 1918
21 ¼ x 21 ¾ inches
Private Collection, New York

THE FIRST HEPATICAS, 1918
22 x 27¾ inches

This catalog was issued April tenth
nineteen thirty, by the Trustees of The
Museum of Modern Art, in New
York. One thousand copies.

PLANDOME PRESS, INC., NEW YORK

Heat. 1919. Oil, 50 x 36½″. Collection Miss Ettie Stettheimer.
This picture of the artist and her sisters with their mother commemorates the latter's birthday.

HENRY McBRIDE

florine Stettheimer

THE MUSEUM OF MODERN ART

acknowledgment and lenders

The President and Trustees of the Museum of Modern Art wish to thank Mr. Marcel Duchamp for his services as Guest Director of the Florine Stettheimer Exhibition. They also extend their grateful acknowledgment to the following:

For special research and counsel: Miss Ettie Stettheimer, Mr. Carl Van Vechten, Mr. R. Kirk Askew, Jr., Mr. Mark Pagano;

For the loan of paintings to the exhibition: Mr. and Mrs. R. Kirk Askew, Jr., New York; A. Everett Austin, Jr., Hartford, Connecticut; Louis Bouché, New York; Mr. and Mrs. John D. Gordan, New York; Edward James, Laguna Beach, California; Adolfo Best-Maugard, Mexico, D. F.; Mrs. Huddleston Rogers, Claremont, Virginia; Miss Ettie Stettheimer, New York; Pavel Tchelitchew, New York; Virgil Thomson, New York; Carl Van Vechten, New York.

Newark Museum, Newark, New Jersey; The United States Military Academy, West Point, New York.

An American Place, New York; Durlacher Brothers, New York.

trustees of the museum of modern art

contents

color plates

Florine Stettheimer

florine stettheimer

"All things counter, original, spare, strange:
Whatever is fickle, freckled (who knows how)
With swift, slow; sweet, sour; adazzle, dim;
He fathers-forth whose beauty is past change:
Praise Him."

Gerard Manley Hopkins

I

Fame is the most uncertain garment man assumes. No one knows exactly how to acquire it, nor how to keep it once acquired. There are instances of some who have striven to avoid it—unsuccessfully. There are others who have spent fortunes in the effort to attain it—with equal unsuccess. Who is the most famous person alive today? I know, but I won't tell you, for before the words may be put into print he may be buried in obloquy. How long does fame last? There is Homer, of course. There are also Byron and Shelley but already more people read their piquant biographies than their so-called deathless verse. And Sir Walter! Who reads the Waverley novels? Yet oceans of ink were once spilled in their praise. The obscure Walt Whitman wrote anonymous letters to the Press attacking his own poetry knowing that to be "one of the ways"; but in the late years of the old man's life Richard Watson Gilder, just to be nice, used to print occasional couplets by Walt in the *Century Magazine,* couplets which were immediately reprinted in the newspapers with mocking comments much like those leveled today at the work of Gertrude Stein. Fame is a most uncertain garment. Yet fame, apparently, is what the Museum of Modern Art now desires for the late Florine Stettheimer.

Family Portrait #1. 1915. Oil on canvas, 40 x 62″. Collection Miss Ettie Stettheimer.

II

Miss Stettheimer died in May 1944 unrecognized as an artist by the world at large. There were no obituaries in the newspapers. Museums as a rule exist upon reputations ready-made but this time it starts to make one. The occasion, therefore, is unusual. In fact, in my experience, it is unprecedented.

Miss Stettheimer's semi-obscurity was not so much due to the public's indifference as to her own. Hers is not a tale of hardship or neglect. She and her two sisters, Miss Carrie and Miss Ettie, presided over a salon that had considerable to do with shaping the intellectual and artistic impulses of the period just past, al.—though at the dinners and receptions which followed in quick succession in their house and in which hardy ideas were put into words which echoed sooner or later in other parts of the city, she seemed often a furtive guest rather than one of the genii loci which she undoubtedly was, for her demure presence invariably counted. The artists who came to these parties came there because of her, most of them in the *avant garde*, such as Gaston Lachaise, Charles Demuth, Pavel Tchelitchew, et al., but all the others in attendance, the writers, singers, dancers, and sometimes even scientists, were definitely interested and amused by Florine's paintings from the

10

moment they first became aware of them. Although this certainly did not constitute fame it was just as certainly not neglect. She had a numerous and faithful following and it was consciousness of this doubtless that lent her the authority that soon appeared in her work and emboldened her to perfect the highly original style which the public is now called upon to appraise.

This style was at first "regular." That is to say she painted in the open-brush-stroke manner derived from the Frans Hals, Velasquez, John Singer Sargent traditions, and which Academicians thirty years ago thought was to be the permanent, final method for painting everything. As employed by Florine in the family portrait which used to hang over the sofa in the small reception room at 58th Street, it brought her somewhere in line with the van Dongen of Paris of those days, but there was already enough freedom and femininity in the work to bar it from the then public exhibitions, femininity when too openly avowed being almost as reprehensible in those days as freedom of expression. For that matter van Dongen himself would not have been any too welcome to those juries.

André Brook. 1915. Oil on canvas, 28 x 34″. Collection Miss Ettie Stettheimer.

11

La Fête à Duchamp. 1917. Oil on canvas, 35 x 45½". Collection Mr. and Mrs. John D. Gordan.

In this picture certain figures are shown as they appear at different stages of the party. Upper left: Marcel Duchamp waves his hand from the automobile driven by Francis Picabia; and in the foreground on the left, they are entering the garden. Facing them, above the archway of flowers: the artist and Albert Gleizes, and seated in the swing, Fania Marinoff. Center, beyond the refreshment table: the artist's sister Carrie and the Marquis de Buenavista. Right, beside the table: Avery Hopwood speaking to Mme Gleizes (Juliette Roche). At the foot of the tree: the artist's sister Ettie with two likenesses of Leo Stein, one on each side. Sprawled on the grass: Picabia and Rocher. Seated on two chairs, side by side: Elizabeth Duncan and Carl Van Vechten. At the supper table on the terrace, the entire party: the artist's sister Ettie proposing a toast on the left, and Marcel Duchamp on the right responding to it.

She did not have to go far in search of subject matter. She looked upon her sisters, her mother and herself as phenomena of surpassing interest (which they indeed were) and did them many times, singly and in groups; and it is possible to surmise that the series of pictures of parties was undertaken more or less as background to an *histoire de famille*, for the "*famille*" pointed up all the compositions, even Mrs. Stettheimer appearing in them, usually aloof and occupied with the

12

game of Russian Bank the while her giddy daughters enacted the rôles of Julie de Lespinasse, Mme du Deffand and Mme de Staël in modern dress.

The artist had not progressed far in this sequence of portraits and party-pictures when it became apparent that she had shaken off the conventional premier-coup of the pseudo-Sargents and had evolved a manner that was to do her for the rest of her painting days. It is not a manner that may be hit off in a word. It might be thought to disdain manner in that it is wilful, unconcerned with precedent and as unpredictable as the flight of a butterfly in a garden of flowers; and yet nothing could be falser than to attribute its effects to lucky accidents. Miss Stettheimer knew what she was doing. She had laws of her own and knew them positively even though she never defined them to herself. She followed her inner impulses with strict integrity and spared nor time nor labor to realize them.* Very early she began to lean heavily upon the use of white pigment. Miss Ettie Stettheimer once remarked to me that she thought a special quality of her sister's work was its power of giving off light. This I, in turn, thought to be due to the artist's lavish, preparatory build-up of Chinese white on the canvas, whites which often were piled up in relief before the actual painting began. Once this got under way I imagine the artist stopped at nothing. She sometimes applied thin tints only partly covering the heavy white base; she sometimes, I suspect, smudged areas of thick paint into smoothness with a cloth, giving it the appearance of a liquid that has been poured on rather than brushed. The actual brushstroke of the usual artist is so seldom employed† in her later works that it suggests a palpable avoidance of "quotations," so confirmed had she become in the habit of doing things in exactly her own way;— but with all these irregularities she was always able to get precision where and when she wanted it. Although she took all the license of a *primitif* she was by no means one herself. Her "line" was a draughtsman's line (she had been a pupil of Kenyon Cox at the Art Students

---

* The following quotation from Florine Stettheimer's diary during early student days in Munich illustrates her continuous inquiry into matters of technique:

"Rafaello came in on us during work this morning. I was glad for I had been experimenting with poor results in a study of the depths of the laurel trees. And had been wishing for some more brilliant medium than casein. He told me to come over and see some of his 'Proben'—as he had been trying for warm depths also. . . . I told him I should follow him. The weather was wretched. . . . But I learned some important things from Schuster-Woldan's experiments. He said I was lucky to just step in and learn the results of ten years of hard work. So I went to Bruggers and got some Copal varnish and hope to get at those laurels tomorrow."

†"I confess to looking at some of the new pictures years ago with scepticism, for there were all sorts of doings in them not to be observed in other artists' work and which looked impermanent. But they have lasted. In the twenty years or so that I have known them I have seen no discoloration of the pigments nor any fading, which is more than I can say for most of the American impressionistic work of the same period."

From the article in *View*, October 1945.

13

Sunday Afternoon in the Country. 1917. Oil on canvas, 50 x 36″. Durlacher Brothers.

Foreground: Edward Steichen photographing Marcel Duchamp, attended by the artist's sister Ettie; Baron de Meyer seated with back turned; Baroness de Meyer under a parasol with Paul Reimers, and the artist's mother playing Patience. Center: Ratan Devi and Adolph Bolm with a parasol. Dr. Arnold Genthe with Mme Bolm; Alfred Seligsberg with arms crossed, the artist's sister Carrie and Albert Sterner with Jo Davidson. Background: left, Marie Sterner watching Paul Thévenaz; right, Paul Chalfin, the Marquis de Buenavista against a tree, and the artist at her easel.

Picnic at Bedford Hills. 1918. Oil on canvas, 40 x 50″. Collection Miss Ettie Stettheimer.
   The artist seated alone with a parasol; her sister Ettie recumbent on a carpet, in conversation with Elie Nadelman; her sister Carrie and Marcel Duchamp setting out the repast.

League), calligraphic, like so much of the best modern "line," and never to be accused of fumbling. Her colors instantly forgot they came from the paint-box and took on the tints of the flowers. When she painted flowers she was never literal in her descriptions of them. The flowers in her flower pieces were, as they were to Odilon Redon, mere points of departure. They are, I believe, sufficiently botanical, but they are also unearthly. I never heard her speak of Redon, and she would not have thought herself related to him, yet there is a kinship between their flowers. Both imbued them with the occult, something reaching out of this world to that other; and of the two, Florine granted them more actual freedom, and the blossoms in her vases wriggled upward with a whimsicality in the stems that is not to be outmatched

15

New York. 1918. Oil on canvas, 60 x 42″. Collection Virgil Thomson.

16

West Point. 1917. Oil on canvas, 45½ x 35½". Collection The United States Military Academy, West Point, N. Y.

This commemorates a visit of the artist, her mother and two sisters in August, 1917.

for waywardness in the "automatic" paintings of Miro. Emerson said somewhere, and I think it is in one of his letters to Carlyle, that he would like the word "whim" engraved over the door to his library. With equal pertinence it could have been engraved over Florine's.

III

The world is full of strangers
They are very strange
I am never going to know them
It is easy to arrange.

F. S.

The only one-man show that Miss Stettheimer permitted herself occurred in the Knoedler Galleries at a time when Marie Sterner was conducting a series of exhibitions there. This was early in her career (1916) before her style had crystallized, before the cathedral pictures and the more important portraits had been painted, and although the press was kind enough in commenting upon it, the attention of the general public was not caught. The artist was vaguely dissatisfied with the exhibition herself and decided that if she ever indulged in a one-man show again it would have to be in a room a little more closely attuned to her special requirements and, preferably, decorated for the occasion by herself. The opportunity for this never materialized. More than one of the dealers expressed a desire to undertake it but each for one reason or another was refused, and in the end Miss Stettheimer began to be regarded by them as "difficult."

Maybe she was. But then she had no real occasion to sell her paintings and when the thing was suggested by her friends as an *événement* natural to the life of an artist, she used to smile and say that she liked her pictures herself and preferred to keep them. At the same time she did lend to public exhibitions, and among them, surprisingly but not inconsistently, to those of the Independent Society where the conditions are exceedingly cruel to anything less than pictures of mural size. But this was a concession to public spirit—of which she had plenty.

In spite of Miss Stettheimer's efforts to protect herself from the clamor of modern activity she was by no means a recluse in the Emily Dickinsonian sense though like that poet she astonished people occasionally by shrewd comments upon phases of existence from which it had been presumed she had been shielded. Details

18

Lake Placid. 1919. Oil, 40 x 50″. Collection Miss Ettie Stettheimer. For identification of persons see contents page.

Asbury Park South. 1920. Oil on canvas, 50 x 60". Collection Miss Ettie Stettheimer.

Looking down from the reviewing stand: Carl Van Vechten. Foreground center: Marcel Duchamp and Fania Marinoff. Right, between park bench and railing: the artist with a parasol. On the beach beyond, in conversation with a sun-burned figure, Avery Hopwood; and Paul Thévenaz photographing. The beach is one segregated for Negroes; and the above-mentioned were led by Carl Van Vechten to interest themselves in the welfare of the Negro race.

in Florine's cathedral pictures recall the mild surprise of Washington legislators at the political acumen displayed in Emily's shy replies to their questions at the dinners to which her father led her during his term as a legislator. The physiognomy of ex-Mayor Jimmy Walker flung up large among the listed glories of the "Cathedral of Broadway" decoration, the wildly comic items in the "Beauty Contest," the beach scene at "Asbury Park," and the frantic excitement of a "Spring Sale" in a pretentious fifty-seventh street dress establishment, are doubly surprising as coming from

21

Beauty Contest: To the memory of P. T. Barnum. 1924. Oil on canvas, 50 x 60″. Collection Miss Ettie Stettheimer.

Upper left: Edward Steichen photographs the contest, with Edna Kenton and the artist looking on.

her. There is nothing malicious in them but a wealth of Puck-like allusions to the foolishness of mankind. The gay familiarity with almost sacrosanct themes, such as Florine's "George Washington" sitting-room annexed to her studio, was something in line, too, with Emily Dickinson's intimacy with Jehovah. George Washington's bust was enshrined in a corner alcove, and I believe there were some statuettes of him here and there, and here hung the "West Point" painting now actually owned by the great military academy up the Hudson. The atmosphere of the little room was patriotic, rather preciously patriotic, but truly patriotic just the same.

22

Spring Sale (At the Dressmaker's). 1921. Oil on canvas, 50 x 40″. Durlacher Brothers.

IV

Then back to New York
And skytowers had begun to grow
And front-stoop houses started to go
And life became quite different
And it was as tho' someone had planted seeds
And people sprouted like common weeds
And seemed unaware of accepted things
And did all sorts of unheard-of things
And out of it grew an amusing thing
Which I think is America having its fling
And what I should like is to paint this thing.

F. S.

The studio itself was one of the curiosities of the town; and very closely related, in appearance, to the work that was done in it. The lofty windows (the studio was double-decked) were hung with billowy cellophane curtains, and the chairs and tables were in white and gold, the tables in glass and gold, and I have a remembrance of lamps screened with white beads and unreal but handsome gilt flowers in the vases. I certainly recall some gilt flowers in a golden bowl on the dining-room table, reinforced by draperies of some golden fabric at the windows.

The windows of the balcony which looked down into the studio were hung with ancient Nottingham lace which incited the ribald to ironic comment; comment, however, which left the artist quite undisturbed, so positive was her affection for lace even in its simplest and least pretentious manifestations. It continually crept into her pictures. It almost became her sign-manual, like the butterfly signature employed by Whistler. It appears in her most serious portrait, that of her mother, painted in 1925. It reappears again and again and finally in the last family group, the one that was exhibited in the Museum of Modern Art's fifteenth anniversary exhibition "*Art in Progress*" in May, 1944, the costumes of Mrs. Stettheimer, Miss Carrie and Miss Ettie all being embellished with lace and only the artist herself renouncing it to wear a severe painting-suit proper for the occasion. It got into the artist's costumes and properties designed for the famous Virgil Thomson—Gertrude Stein opera "Four Saints In Three Acts"; very happily when it was seen that the camera taking a shot at Saint Theresa in the first act was draped with a black lace mantilla, and very dramatically when a lady magnificently got up in black lace

24

Russian Bank. 1921. Oil on canvas, 40 x 36″. Collection Miss Ettie Stettheimer.

Delphinium and Columbine. c.1923. Oil on canvas, 36x 30″. Durlacher Brothers.

makes a sudden appearance to say to Saint Ignatius; "In a minute"; and then
promptly vanishes. So much costume for so little in the way of conversation must
have seemed to Miss Stettheimer the height of extravagance, and wittily absurd in
itself. Certainly it seemed so to the opera's audiences. The "In a minute" got a
rapturous "hand" at every performance I attended.

It was also Miss Stettheimer's original intention to frame in the entire stage
picture with an enormous lace paper frill, much as boxes of candy were decorated
years ago, but she was dissuaded from this. Probably the fire laws did the dissuasion.

This description of the studio is vague, I am afraid, and I have not particularized
its fantasy enough, but anyway those who saw "Four Saints" will easily see the connection between such a studio and the famous stage sets. The atmosphere was alike
in both.

26

Portrait of Marcel Duchamp. 1923. Oil on canvas, 30 x 26″. Collection Miss Ettie Stettheimer.

Portrait of Carl Van Vechten. 1922. Oil on canvas, 28 x 26″. Collection Carl Van Vechten.

Upper left are allusions to the sitter's interests and affections: a café in Paris, the marquee of a theatre with the name of his wife, Fania Marinoff. Above, a figure in white represents Carl Van Vechten as a cook, with the *cordon-bleu*. A piano indicates his activity as a music critic. Upper right: the actress' dressing table with a Japanese print and a Nô mask of Fania Marinoff.

Portrait of Henry McBride. 1922. Oil on canvas, 30 x 26″. Collection Miss Ettie Stettheimer.

The background beyond the tennis courts consists of allusions to various works of art: one of the artist's own flower pieces, a female nude by Gaston Lachaise, a church by Charles Demuth, a watercolor by John Marin, and a marine by Winslow Homer.

V

The designing of these stage sets and costumes marked the artist's first and only venture into the modern world of publicity but it was successful from every point of view; and thoroughly enjoyable to her. The "difficult" Miss Stettheimer was not in the least difficult on this occasion, suggesting that she was not in reality difficult at all but merely aware of the conditions in which her art flourished and this time found them met. All the circumstances connected with the presentation of the opera were ideal and worthy of more prolonged study than is here possible for they brought actors, musicians and artists into the same sort of collaboration that produced the Diaghileff ballet successes in Paris; and it is odd, seeing how frantically eager the New York theatre is to be thought artistic, that none of its impresarios have since inquired into the process by which "Four Saints" so definitely got that way.

The first happy accident connected with the affair was the fact that the composer Virgil Thomson had lived in close communion with the artists of Paris during his stay there and got to know the real ones from the spurious. His admiration for Florine's work was instantaneous, occurring on his first visit to the studio, and it seemed to be settled at once that she would be the inevitable artist for the décor, were Heaven to be kind enough to permit so unusual and delightful event as the presentation of this opera to occur; and she in turn had such complete faith in

Self Portrait. 1923. Oil on canvas, 40 x 26″. Collection Miss Ettie Stettheimer.

4 Saints in 3 Acts. Act I.

"An Opera to be Sung." Scenery and costumes by Florine Stettheimer (executed by Kate Drain Lawson); Book by Gertrude Stein; Scenario by Maurice Grosser; Music by Virgil Thomson (conducted by Alexander Smallens); Choreography by Frederick Ashton; Production by John Houseman. First produced by The Friends and Enemies of Modern Music at the Wadsworth Atheneum, Hartford, Connecticut, February 8, 1934.

Virgil's judgment that when Heaven did finally relent and say, "Get on with it," the discussions as to details between the two of them were always easy.

The next happy accident—and this is most important and has never been sufficiently descanted upon—was the decision of A. Everett Austin to do the opera in the Hartford Atheneum's theatre of which he was then the director, for Mr. Austin was an ardent enthusiast for baroque art and was generally credited with the emphasis his museum laid upon this form of expression. Just how far along the rehearsals had progressed before the entire company (including singers, dancers, musicians, costumers, and of course Mr. Smallens the orchestra leader, Mr. Thomson the composer, Freddy Ashton the English choreographer and the marvelous electrician Mr. Feder) migrated to Hartford for the finish, I do not know, but I do know that the last-minute improvisations, occurring as they did in a museum and with all the contributors drinking in ideas from the baroque masterpieces that surrounded them,

32

4 Saints in 3 Acts.
St. Theresa II, Bruce Howard; St. Theresa I, Beatrice Robinson Wayne; St. Ignatius, Edward Matthews

were of inestimable value to the production. That is the point I should particularly like to have made clear to Broadway—not necessarily that all opera productions should be fabricated in museums but that the museums should be used as consultants and that the artists employed should be real ones.

The première was a howling success, for the opera, for the singers, for the entrancing stage-pictures. I don't recall a readier reception for a new piece either in America or abroad. It is true the audience was a bit special. It had been recruited from all over yet everybody seemed to know everybody and that gave it peculiar charm. Half of them were of the *avant garde*, aware that a Gertrude Stein opera was about as advanced as anyone could ever hope to get in this world and fully persuaded, even before the curtain went up, that the evening could not possibly be a failure. One would laugh either against Gertrude or with her. One, in any case, would laugh. Whatever stage-fright there may have been about the theatre, it was certainly not in evidence out front.

When the curtain went up—or rather, was "pulled apart," for the little Atheneum theatre is very chic—there was a gasp of astonishment and delight. This *avant garde* after all knew something about pictures and could see at once that the saint kneeling in front and clad in voluminous purple silks was quite as ecstatic as anything El Greco had ever devised in that line, and that the costumes of the two Saint Theresas and the other saints, as well as the effects produced by the cellophane background and the remarkable lighting bestowed upon them by Mr. Feder, were all addressed to the painter-like eye. They felt at home at once with that sort of thing; unlike Mr. George Jean Nathan whose disgust with the opening refrain, "It makes it well fish," was not theirs. They knew the jargon of the artists and something of the jargon of the saints, and "It makes it well fish" recalled to them the ancient symbolic fish of the sarcophagi, standing for the sanctity that is so notably a preoccupation with saints. It seldom paid to quarrel with Gertrude's locutions. She usually knew what she was about. Even the matter of the two Saint Theresas (Virgil Thomson's solution to one of his musical problems) could be defended. When the dispute about this was at its height I met Mrs. W. Murray Crane at one of the New York performances who said: "Why such a fuss? After all, some of the leading authorities hold that there was something dual in Saint Theresa's nature." The Hartford audience was better prepared for these matters than the New York critics were to be later on when the show was transferred to the big Forty-Fourth Street Theatre, but they paid less attention to the Gertrude Stein words, at first, than they did to the Stettheimer sets which they avidly "ate up," as the phrase goes, until the absurd interruption of the strutting Compère and Commère awakened their ears as their eyes had been previously by the costumes, and they sat back comfortably in their chairs to listen to the fantastic dialogue, definitely laughing with Gertrude rather than at her, and definitely enchanted with Virgil Thomson's music and Florine Stettheimer's colors.

During the first entr'act and whilst the heroes and heroines of the occasion were taking curtain calls to the accompaniment of cheers (the shrinking violet Miss Stettheimer taking a solo bow in her turn with extreme nonchalance) I dashed backstage just in time to see this violet being ardently embraced by Freddy Ashton the

34

Family Portrait No. 2. 1933. Oil, 46 x 64½". Collection Miss Ettie Stettheimer. Left to right: the artist, her sister Ettie, her mother, and her sister Carrie.

Tulips under a Canopy. c.1925. Oil on canvas, 40 x 32″. Collection Mrs. Huddleston Rogers.

choreographer, both of them in the kind of heaven that only artists know, at the way things were going; and I could not resist the thought that for Florine this was genuinely a coming-out party. She came out indeed but she stayed out only for the duration of this opera. She took an enormous amount of innocent satisfaction in her contribution to it and I have the idea that she scarcely missed a performance of the work. Even during the last days of the run, when the piece had been transferred to the Empire Theatre, she had constructed at her own expense a decorative gadget of stars and symbols that swung in the air above the last scene and made it to her mind, and to mine too, distinctly more "well fish." But I suppose Mr. George Jean Nathan never will understand this. We can't all be symbolists.

37

Portrait of My Mother. 1925. Oil on canvas, 38¼ x 26¼". Collection Miss
Ettie Stettheimer.

Portrait of My Sister, Ettie Stettheimer. 1923. Oil on canvas, 40⅜ x
26¼″. Collection Miss Ettie Stettheimer.

VI

Miss Stettheimer's best portrait, in my opinion, is the one of her mother. This is
eminently fitting in the case of an artist whose horizons for such a long time were
kept within the limits of her own home. It is an idealized portrait done with great
tenderness and love and yet touched with irrepressible wit. I call it witty the way the
straggling carnations break the severe blacks of the piano. I think it witty the way
the palm-leaves venture into the composition and the way in which the laces frame
in the mother's dream-picture of her children in the background. The mother's
faintly bewildered but uncomplaining expression as she thinks of these children is
witty, too. It is a true apotheosis; and it is a picture, I believe, that will take permanent rank in the not too great an array of distinguished American portraits.

Natatorium Undine. 1927. Oil on canvas, 50 x 60". Collection Miss Ettie Stettheimer.

Upper left: Fania Marinoff at the table, and the artist with a parasol. Seated along the edge of the pool in a striped bathing dress: the artist's sister, Ettie.

The same amused insight characterizes the portraits of her sisters and gives curious incandescence to the family group pictures, and notably to the last one, the one that was being shown in this Museum at the time of the artist's death. I had occasion then to remark upon it in my review of the exhibition for the New York Sun, and as what I said remains my opinion, here it is:

"It is fragile, with the fragility of a flower but it also has the authority of a flower. The artist herself is seen, in painting garb, on a lofty city terrace, with her two sisters and her mother, and in the distance the Chrysler Tower which always seems as though it might itself have been a Stettheimer creation, looms like something in the Arabian night. The whole picture, in fact, is an Arabian Nights' Entertainment; very exquisite, very charming, and if you wish to be reassured on that point, very exact as to the likenesses."

That last quoted phrase, no doubt, should be qualified. It applies to the family portraits but not to those of outsiders. She could take all sorts of liberties with her own people but never departed from the resemblances. No matter how slight the reference to a Stettheimer it was always recognizable. The drawings of the mother,

Fourth of July #1. 1927. Oil on canvas, 28 x 18″. Collection Mrs. Huddleston Rogers.

Portrait of My Sister, Carrie W. Stettheimer. 1923. Oil on canvas, 37½ x 25½″
Collection Miss Ettie Stettheimer.

42

often in the background of the recorded party-activities of the daughters, are more "like" than any photograph of the lady could have been. The study of Miss Ettie, groomed like one of Scheherazade's heroines, reclining beside a Christmas tree ablaze with lights and searching the starry heavens, wide-eyed, for the mystery of life, is as happy a blend of her worldliness and spirituality as any psychiatrist could ask for. Miss Carrie's portrait is less fortunate. The intention is again playful but the result is slightly operatic. If she had that side it was not always visible to all of her friends. The portraits of the artist's "Aunt Caroline" and of her teacher "Fräulein von Preiser of Stuttgart" also suggest opera but obviously what laughter there is is leveled less at the personages than at the vanished fashions they were called upon to illustrate.

VII

New York
At last grown young
With noise
And colour
And light
And jazz
Dance marathons and poultry shows
Soul-savings and rodeos
Gabfests and beauty contests
Skytowers and bridal showers
Speak-easy bars and motor cars
Columnists and movie stars.

F. S.

When it came to the portraits of "outsiders" the joke was more important than the resemblance. Among those thus immortalized were Carl Van Vechten, Marcel Duchamp, Virgil Thomson, Louis Bouché, Baron de Meyer, Joseph Hergesheimer and the writer of this essay. Of these portraits the most whimsical is the one of Marcel Duchamp.

"*There was nothing accidental in this,*" I wrote in an account published last October in "View," "*for Marcel in real life is pure fantasy. If you were to study his paintings and particularly his art-constructions, and were then to try to conjure up his physical appearance, you could not fail to guess him, for he is his own best creation, and exactly what you thought.*

43

Portrait of Alfred Stieglitz. 1928. Oil on canvas, 38 x 25½″. An American Place.

Here and there in the background, appear names of artists represented by Alfred Stieglitz, notably: John Marin; Marsden Hartley; Arthur Dove; Paul Strand; and Georgia O'Keeffe. Behind Stieglitz is a view of Lake George, where he lived.

44

My Birthday Eyegay. 1929. Oil
on canvas, 38 x 26″. Collection
Edward James.

In the portrait he is something of a Pierrot perched aloft upon a Jack-in-Box contraption which he is surreptitiously manipulating to gain greater heights for his apotheosis. Among the 'outside' portraits this is the best from the point of view of pure painting. It is also the simplest. The most complicated character in the whole range of contemporary art has been reduced to one transparent equation."

It is scarcely necessary to explain that these highly imaginative portraits did not depend upon actual sittings.

"I suppose I came nearer to sitting than most of the others," to continue with the article in "View," *"for my portrait originated during a house-party given by the Stettheimers in a Seabright cottage many years ago and one evening I detected the artist over in one corner of the salon furtively jotting down, presumably, some of my lineaments, but I was not permitted to see what hieroglyphics she had acquired nor how many—but they must have been few. At the time of this house-party the Seabright lawn-tennis tournament was in progress and as I was in those days something of a player and mad about the game I went over each afternoon to see what the sensational new Frenchmen, Borotra, Cochet and Lacoste (then playing for the first time in*

45

Cathedrals of Broadway. 1929. Oil on canvas, 60 x 50″. Collection Miss Ettie Stettheimer.

Lower left corner, entering the night club: the artist in a black coat, her sister, and Stella Wanger, accompanied by the latter's son.

Three Flowers and a Dragonfly.
1928. Oil on canvas, 30 x 26".
Collection A. Everett Austin, Jr.

America) were doing. When my portrait made its debut the next winter I was as much astonished as anybody else to find myself seated in the picture against a background of a tennis tournament in full progress. Up above in the sky were references to my aesthetic preoccupations, such as a hint of the celebrated palm-tree watercolor by Winslow Homer, the statue of a "Woman" by Gaston Lachaise, a watercolor by John Marin and so on but the heavy emphasis on tennis in the picture was something that I had to explain away to many critics. I scarcely yet have lived it down.

"The heavy emphasis in the Carl Van Vechten portrait is laid, properly enough, on books; two heavy tomes occupying the foreground, one of them being the already classic 'Tiger in the House'—but in spite of these products of a mature mind Miss Stettheimer preferred to take an ageless view of the author and portrayed him as a guileless youth. She rejected age in all of her friends for that matter and in the portraits turned us into the essences of what we were. The 'too, too solid flesh' meant nothing to her. She weighed the spirit. She knew very well that Mr. Van Vechten frequented cafés both in Paris and in New York, and said so in the picture—but apparently she did not hold it against him."

47

Cathedrals of Wall Street. 1939. Oil on canvas, 60 x 50″. Collection Miss Ettie Stettheimer.

Lower left, holding up the dedicatory pennant: the artist. At the foot of the statue of George Washington: Grace Moore about to sing. Foreground, in the center: Mrs. Franklin D. Roosevelt, escorted by Fiorello H. LaGuardia, Michael Ericson in an American Legion uniform, Michael J. Sullivan—a Civil War veteran, Clagett Wilson and an Indian chief.

48

Cathedrals of Fifth Avenue. 1931. Oil, 60 x 50″. Collection Miss Ettie Stettheimer.
For identification of persons see contents page.

VIII

The unloved painting;

I was pure white
You made a painted show-thing of me
You called me the real-thing

Your creation
No setting was too good for me
Silver—even gold
I needed gorgeous surroundings
You then sold me to another man.

F. S.

With this posthumous exhibition in the Museum of Modern Art the trial by the public of Miss Stettheimer's work begins. I have no doubt whatever but that it will win permanent regard. It has a spirited and original style. It is not a case, as so often happens, of borrowing from European sources. It is strictly native. It has our special way of making fun of things, of getting rid of formality and stiffness and testifying to affection through light-heartedness. It is that necessity we have of calling our great men by their first names, of reducing everything to one level, of being—in a word—democratic. It is this quality that has already caught the attention of the foreign artists who have seen it, such as Pavel Tchelitchew, Marcel Duchamp, and just lately Christian Bérard. They rate it among their most interesting "finds" in America and relish its accent exceedingly.

Now what pleases the "discerning few" can please the general if the general be given a chance at it. In art, as in religion, the public finally arrives at the true values. You remember in *The Brothers Karamazoff* the old priest's dying admonition to the younger men: "Give them the Bible. Do not think they will not understand." Nothing that is worth while is above the public comprehension. There are no closed doors to opinion and certainly there is no class distinction in thought. "What Plato has thought you can think." Shelley told one of his friends that he "wrote for only six people." Gertrude Stein told me personally in 1914 "but I'd like to be acknowledged and have my books on the bookshelves like other writers." At a time when no one else in England thought much of William Blake, Charles Lamb said: "But there really is something great in 'Tiger, tiger burning bright.'" The six people who believed in Shelley, the six who believed in Gertrude, the six who believed in Blake have all had followers. The first step in the process of acquiring fame is to obtain the six believers. These Florine Stettheimer had. We will shortly be able to estimate their leavening power.

HENRY McBRIDE

51

Cathedrals of Art (unfinished). 1942. Oil on canvas, 60 x 50″. Collection Miss Ettie Stettheimer.
For identification of persons see opposite page.

52

The first three writers to get into print effectively on the subject of Miss Stettheimer's work were Carl Van Vechten, Paul Rosenfeld and Penelope Redd, of the Pittsburgh Sunday Post. Mr. Van Vechten and Mr. Rosenfeld were friends of the artist and favorably placed to know of her work from the beginning; Miss Redd rather remarkably recognized its qualities from a single example. Here are excerpts from their appraisals.

In The Reviewer, February 1922, Mr. Van Vechten wrote:

"I pause in wonder, also, before the canvases of Florine Stettheimer, canvases as gay as the fête at Neuilly. Her bowls of multi-coloured zinnias, fox-gloves and stocks are lacking in perversity. These are not the flowers of Demuth. They are apparently more honest, but no clairvoyant spirit standing before them would be misled by their honesty. Ecstasy is there but it is agathodemonic and not kakodemonic. It is perhaps, however, in her riotous picnics and parties, flooded with sunlight and splashes of violent colour that Miss Stettheimer is most original. This lady has got into her painting a very modern quality, the quality that ambitious American musicians will have to get into their compositions before anyone will listen to them. At the risk of being misunderstood, I must call this quality jazz. Jazz music, indubitably, is an art in itself, but before a contemporary American can triumph in the serious concert halls he must reproduce not the thing itself but its spirit in a more lasting form. This, Miss Stettheimer has abundantly succeeded in doing."

Mr. Rosenfeld wrote in The Nation, May 4, 1932:

"These brilliant canvases of hers do resemble gay decorations in coloured paper, and lacquered red and blue glass balls, and gilt-foil stars, and crêpe streamers, and angels of cotton wadding, and tinted wax tapers. That is because she has a highly refined decorative sense combined with a certain predilection for the ornamental, the frivolous, the festive; indeed a sense of the poetry and humour and pathos of what is merely embellishing. Many of her graceful, delicate shapes are imitated from festoonery, plumage, tassels, rosettes, fringes, bouquets, and all kinds of old-fashioned trappings. Others are in the forms of some Oriental elfin world in which everything is sinuous, diminutive and tendril-like; and huge bees and dragonflies and glorified insects and all sorts of non-human, vermicular, and winged creatures are the norm. She seems to delight in garish, tinselly, glittering colours; the colours of 'paste' and bric-a-brac and paper flowers; and induces her paint to form tiny sparkling brilliants. It is a fabulous little world of two-dimensional shapes with which she entertains us; but beautifully, sharply, deliciously felt; and perfectly communicative of the pleasure with which it was created."

In the Pittsburgh Sunday Post, May 11, 1924, Miss Redd said:

"Florine Stettheimer invents a new mode of expressing symbolism as original as the Chinese in this painting (a garden scene entitled 'Russian Bank'). She makes her garden not by the facts already described but in the superbly painted bouquet of flowers placed on a table, which makes a dazzling focus for the observer's eye. Miss Stettheimer is the only woman painter in America, and indeed there would seem to be few elsewhere who project an individual point of view on canvas. She carries the art of painting to its completest power in expressing a number of incidents occurring simultaneously. . . . Miss Stettheimer, more than any other painter whom we know, has developed a symbolic and decorative type of painting that also engages us by its human interest."

Cathedrals of Art. Opposite page.

In the foreground, left and right: Compère and Commère, Robert Locher and the artist. On the left, at the foot of the column inscribed "Art in America": A. Everett Austin, Jr.; and behind him on the right, Julien Levy and R. Kirk Askew, Jr., and on the left, with hand flung up, Pavel Tchelitchew. Seated in the upper left corner amid paintings by Picasso, Mondrian and Rousseau: Alfred H. Barr, Jr. The painting in the rear is by Frans Hals whom the artist admired. Standing in the upper right, in front of a sculptured figure by Gertrude Vanderbilt is Juliana Force. Lower right, at the foot of the column inscribed "American Art," with small flags marked Stop and Go: Henry McBride. Left of the column: Monroe Wheeler and two unidentified figures. Center foreground, adored by an anonymous female art lover, an infant personifying the state of the arts in this country, in an effulgence of spotlights, being photographed by George Platt Lynes. On steps: left, Alfred Stieglitz; right, holding a bust by Elie Nadelman, Marie Sterner. At the head of the stairs, with children: Francis Henry Taylor and Harry B. Wehle.

catalog

In dimensions height precedes width. An asterisk (*) before the title indicates that the work is illustrated. Unless otherwise noted the following paintings are lent by Miss Ettie Stettheimer, New York.

Landscape. c. 1914. Oil on canvas, 29 x 36".

*André Brook (rear view). 1915. Oil on canvas, 28 x 34". Ill. p. 11.

*Family Portrait #1. 1915. Oil on canvas, 40 x 62". Ill. p. 10.

Flowers Against Blue-Green. c. 1915. Oil on canvas, 30 x 40".

Flowers Against Wallpaper. c. 1915. Oil on canvas, 36 x 26".

Tulips. c. 1916. Oil on canvas, 30 x 36". Lent by Durlacher Brothers, New York.

*La Fête à Duchamp. 1917. Oil on canvas, 35 x 45½". Lent by Mr. and Mrs. John D. Gordan, New York. Ill. p. 12.

*Sunday Afternoon in the Country. 1917. Oil on canvas, 50 x 36". Lent by Durlacher Brothers, New York. Ill. p. 14.

*West Point. 1917. Oil on canvas, 45½ x 35½". Lent by The United States Military Academy, West Point, New York. Ill. p. 17.

*Heat. 1918. Oil on canvas, 50 x 36½". Color frontispiece.

*New York. 1918. Oil on canvas, 60 x 42". Lent by Virgil Thomson, New York. Ill. p. 16.

*Picnic at Bedford Hills. 1918. Oil on canvas, 40 x 50". Ill. p. 15.

*Lake Placid. 1919. Oil on canvas, 40 x 50". Color plate, p. 19.

*Asbury Park South. 1920. Oil on canvas, 50 x 60". Ill. p. 21.

Portrait of Adolfo Best-Maugard. c. 1920? Oil on canvas, 28 x 18". Lent by Adolfo Best-Maugard, Mexico, D. F.

*Spring Sale (At the Dressmaker's). 1921. Oil on canvas, 50 x 40". Lent by Durlacher Brothers, New York. Ill. p. 23.

Still Life with Flowers. 1921. Oil on canvas, 26 x 30".

Flowers in a Cup. 1921. Oil on canvas, 25 x 30". Lent by The Newark Museum, Newark, New Jersey.

Flower Bouquet #1. c. 1921. Watercolor, 20½ x 29".

Flower Bouquet #2. c. 1921. Watercolor, 19½ x 24½".

*Russian Bank. 1921. Oil on canvas, 40 x 36". Ill. p. 25.

*Portrait of Carl Van Vechten. 1922. 28 x 26". Lent by Carl Van Vechten, New York. Ill. p. 28.

*Portrait of Henry McBride. 1922. Oil on canvas, 30 x 26". Ill. p. 29.

Portrait of Baron de Meyer. 1923. Oil on canvas, 38 x 26". Lent by Durlacher Brothers, New York.

Portrait of Joseph Hergesheimer. 1923. Oil on canvas, 30 x 26".

Portrait of Louis Bouché. 1923. Oil on canvas, 28 x 18". Lent by Louis Bouché, New York.

*Portrait of Marcel Duchamp. 1923. Oil on canvas, 30 x 26". Ill. p. 27.

*Portrait of my Sister, Ettie Stettheimer. 1923. Oil on canvas, 40⅜ x 26¼". Ill. p. 39.

*Portrait of my Sister, Carrie W. Stettheimer. 1923. Oil on canvas, 37½ x 25½". Ill. p. 42.

*Self Portrait. 1923. Oil on canvas, 40 x 26". Ill. p. 31.

*Delphinium and Columbine. c. 1923. Oil on canvas, 36 x 30". Lent by Durlacher Brothers, New York. Ill. p. 26.

*Beauty Contest: To the memory of P. T. Barnum. 1924. Oil on canvas, 50 x 60". Ill. p. 22.

*Portrait of my Mother. 1925. Oil on canvas, 38¼ x 26¼". Ill. p. 38.

*Tulips under a Canopy. c. 1925. Oil on canvas, 40 x 32″. Lent by Mrs. Huddleston Rogers, Claremont, Virginia. *Ill. p. 37.*

*Fourth of July #1. 1927. Oil on canvas, 28 x 18″. Lent by Mrs. Huddleston Rogers, Claremont, Virginia. *Ill. p. 41.*

Fourth of July #2. 1927. Oil on canvas, 28 x 18″. Lent by Durlacher Brothers, New York.

*Natatorium Undine. 1927. Oil on canvas, 50 x 60″. *Ill. p. 40.*

*Portrait of Alfred Stieglitz. 1928. Oil on canvas, 38 x 25½″. Lent by An American Place, New York. *Ill. p. 44.*

Portrait of Father Hoff. 1928. Oil on canvas, 28 x 18″.

Portrait of my Aunt, Caroline Walter Neustater. 1928. Oil on canvas, 37½ x 25½″.

*Three Flowers and a Dragonfly. 1928. Oil on canvas, 30 x 26″. Lent by A. Everett Austin, Jr., Hartford, Connecticut. *Ill. p. 47.*

*Cathedrals of Broadway. 1929. Oil on canvas, 60 x 50″. *Ill. p. 46.*

*My Birthday Eyegay. 1929. Oil on canvas, 38 x 26″. Lent by Edward James, Laguna Beach, California. *Ill. p. 45.*

Portrait of our Nurse, Margaret Burgess. 1929. Oil on canvas, 38 x 20″.

Portrait of my Teacher in Stuttgart, Fräulein von Preiser. 1929. Oil on canvas, 38 x 20″. Lent by Durlacher Brothers, New York.

Love Flight of a Pink Candy Heart. 1930. Oil on canvas, 60 x 40″.

*Cathedrals of Fifth Avenue. 1931. Oil on canvas, 60 x 50″. *Color plate, p. 49.*

Sun. 1931. Oil on canvas, 38 x 26″. Lent by Pavel Tchelitchew, New York.

Flowers with a Snake. 1932. Oil on canvas, 29½ x 25½″. Lent by Mr. and Mrs. R. Kirk Askew, Jr., New York.

*Family Portrait #2. 1933. Oil on canvas, 46 x 64½″. *Color plate, p. 35.*

*Cathedrals of Wall Street. 1939. Oil on canvas, 60 x 50″. *Ill. p. 48.*

*Cathedrals of Art (unfinished). 1942. Oil on canvas, 60 x 50″. *Ill. p. 52.*

bibliography

American art annual, volume XIV. p616. Washington, D. C., American federation of arts, 1917.

Brief listing in *Who's Who in Art.*

American society of painters, sculptors and gravers. New York, Whitney museum of American art, 1932.

Catalog of an exhibition held Feb 6-28, listing one painting by Stettheimer.

Art in a doll house. Art digest v20,no7,p8 Jan 1 1946.

Includes photographic miniature of Florine's portrait of her sister Carrie.

Arts council of the City of New York. One hundred important paintings by living American artists. p74-5 New York, 1929.

Catalog of an exhibition held Apr 15-27.

Carnegie institute, Pittsburgh. Twenty-third annual international exhibition of painting. 1934.

Catalog of an exhibition held Apr 24-June 15, listing one painting by Stettheimer.

Colony club, New York. Modern sculpture, watercolors and drawings. 1922.

Catalog of an exhibition held Apr 2-13, listing one painting by Stettheimer.

Du Bois, Guy Pène. The American society of painters, sculptors and gravers. Creative Art v10,p131-5 Feb 1932.

Comment on the 11th annual at the Whitney museum, headed by a reproduction of Stettheimer's *Cathedrals of Broadway.*

Flint, Ralph. Lily lady goes west. Town & Country p64 Jan 1943.

Hartley, Marsden. The paintings of Florine Stettheimer. 4 illus Creative Art v9,p18-23 July 1931.

Knoedler, M. & Co., New York. American paintings and sculpture pertaining to the war. [1918]

Catalog of an exhibition held Apr 29-May 15, listing one painting by Stettheimer.

McBride, Henry. [Accounts of *Four Saints in Three Acts* by Gertrude Stein] New York Sun Feb 24, Feb 28, Nov 16 1934.

————Florine Stettheimer: a reminiscence. 5 illus View ser5,no3,p13-15 Oct 1945.

————The museums reopen. New York Sun May 27 1944.

Review of the 15th anniversary show at the Museum of Modern Art, with special comment on Stettheimer's *Family Portrait*.

————The three Miss Stettheimers. Town & Country Dec 1946?

Scheduled for publication this winter.

[Magazine cover by Florine Stettheimer] Town & Country May 1945.

Miss Florine Stettheimer [obituary] New York Times p46 May 14 1944.

Modern artists of America, incorporated, New York. Exhibition by members. New York, Joseph Brummer galleries, 1922.

Catalog of an exhibition held Apr 1-30, listing one painting by Stettheimer.

New York. Museum of modern art. Art in our time. plate 135 New York, 1939.

Catalog of an exhibition held May 10-Sept 30.

————Art in progress. p108,224 New York, 1944.

Catalog of an exhibition held May 24-Oct 15.

————Modern works of art. p34, plate 48 New York, 1934.

Catalog of an exhibition held Nov 20 1934-Jan 20 1935.

————20th century portraits, by Monroe Wheeler. p24, plate 80 New York, 1942.

Catalog of exhibition held Dec 9 1942-Jan 24 1943.

No-Jury society of artists, Chicago. First annual exhibition. Chicago, 1922.

Catalog of an exhibition held Oct 2-16 at the galleries of Marshall Field, listing two paintings by Stettheimer.

Rosenfeld, Paul. Florine Stettheimer. Accent v5,no2,p99-102 Winter 1945.

————The world of Florine Stettheimer. The Nation v134,p522-3 May 4 1932.

Society of independent artists, New York. [Annual exhibition catalogs] New York, 1917-26.

One or two paintings regularly exhibited by Florine Stettheimer.

Van Vechten, Carl. Pastiches et pistaches. v2,no4,p270 The Reviewer Feb 1922.

Wanamaker gallery of modern decorative art, New York. Annual American exhibition. 1923.

Catalog of an exhibition held Jan 22-Feb 17, listing one painting by Stettheimer, with color illustration on cover.

————Second annual decorative exhibition. [1924?]

Catalog of an exhibition held Mar 1-21, listing two paintings by Stettheimer.

Whitney museum of American art, New York. First biennial exhibition of contemporary American painting. New York, 1932.

Catalog of an exhibition held Nov. 22 1932-Jan 5 1933, listing one painting by Stettheimer.

Zatkin, Nathan, ed. Four saints in three acts. New York, Aaronson & Cooper, 1934.

Souvenir book with illustrations, including essay by Carl Van Vechten.

Ten thousand copies of this book have been printed in September, 1946, for the Trustees of the Museum of Modern Art by the Plantin Press, New York. The color inserts were printed by the Litho-Krome Company, Columbus, Georgia.

Franklin C.
WATKINS

by Andrew Carnduff Ritchie

The Museum of Modern Art
New York

ACKNOWLEDGMENTS

On behalf of the President and Trustees of the Museum of Modern Art the director of the exhibition wishes to thank the collectors and museums whose generosity in lending has made the exhibition possible. Particular thanks are due to Mr. Henry P. McIlhenny for his great kindness in permitting us to borrow his two large paintings, *Death* and *Resurrection*, at no small inconvenience to himself; to Mr. Frank K. M. Rehn, Mr. Watkins' dealer, for his assistance in connection with all the details of the exhibition; to the *Magazine of Art* for permission to reprint excerpts from an article by Franklin C. Watkins; and to the artist himself who has been of inestimable help in the preparation of the catalog. I also wish to thank Miss Alice Bacon and Miss Margaret Miller for their assistance in preparing the exhibition and the catalog.

ANDREW CARNDUFF RITCHIE
Director of the Exhibition

CONTENTS

Color Plates

Misses Maude and Maxine Meyer de Schauensee, 1941   *frontispiece*
Oil, 50 x 40⅛". Collection Mr. and Mrs. Rodolphe Meyer de Schauensee,
Devon, Pa.

Resurrection, 1947-48   *facing page* 38
Oil and tempera, 9' x 14'4". Collection Henry P. McIlhenny,
Philadelphia, Pa.

The artist painting the portrait of Justice Owen J. Roberts, 1947

Franklin C.
WATKINS

Paint may order life and increase it;
but it is paint, and must stay paint
and reduce life to painted terms.
FRANKLIN C. WATKINS

Watkins is a painter. All his life he has courted paint to its advantage and
to his. He draws with paint; he thinks, feels, even smiles with paint. By
nature warm and sensitive, he has a poetic imagination that abstracts a com-
pelling image from the merest suggestion and the most unlikely material:
death in an orchard, a fire eater at a circus, a man playing solitaire, a Supreme
Court judge.

He is a serious painter, much concerned with the nature of his materials.
He is a modern painter with a healthy respect for the traditions of his craft.
He is above all a colorist who has derived inspiration unashamedly from many
sources. As he has said to his students: "Influence is inevitable, so best find
good company for a little while — you'll be alone soon enough." He has
been "alone" for many years now and he has made his own distinctive contribution to American painting. With elegance and a characteristic fancifulness
and humor he has uncovered a particular strain of the American temperament
and one that has never been so well expressed before.

Born in New York, he was brought up in North Carolina, educated in part
in Virginia and finally in Philadelphia where he has lived most of his working
life. He was a pupil at the Pennsylvania Academy of the Fine Arts in the
latter city, a venerable institution that has given us many fine painters, among
them Eakins, Demuth and Marin. But most of all he is an adopted son of
Philadelphia itself, a city with perhaps a longer history of artistic production
than any other in America.

His training at the Academy was severely academic and, as he tells us himself, the shadow of Eakins' pictorial precepts hung like a pall over him and
his fellow students. As students will, they rebelled from the strict discipline
in anatomy that was Eakins' legacy to the school, and determined to follow
instead the new freedom of color and form, discovered by post-impressionists
like Gauguin, Lautrec and Cézanne, which was carried to a higher pitch of
intensity by Matisse and his followers. Following this revolt of his student

5

days, Watkins, having won two travelling fellowships, studied abroad in Spain, France and Italy. The Venetians, Giorgione and Tintoretto in particular, and the Venetian-trained El Greco, seem to have impressed him most. The seductiveness of their color, the mannerist or expressionist qualities of their figure drawing and the opulent pictorial architecture of their compositions left a lasting imprint upon his own style.

Watkins has never been a prolific painter, and the first few years in the '20s, after he returned from abroad, were something of a strain. His family suffered financial reverses when he was a student, which forced him to seek work for a time in an advertising agency to earn a living. The few canvases he was able to produce, and the fewer still he was able to sell in those early years might have discouraged a less determined artist. His first portraits and figure compositions, as one might expect, find him searching for a style, trying now one, now another direction until he finds himself securely on his own feet in the early '30s. The portrait of Paul Cret (p. 11), painted in 1922, and the *Still Life* (p. 12) from the following year have a solidity of modelling and an assurance of brushwork that reflect his sound academy training. Despite Watkins' student resentment of the Eakins discipline, the older master has had a hand, one suspects, in the Cret portrait — in its forthrightness of characterization and in the strength of its draughtsmanship. (And Eakins, I feel, remained with him as a perhaps unconscious inspiration for most of his best portraits. Watkins, in fact, came to admire him tremendously in later years.) The *Still Life* has a somewhat academic flavor to it with a suggestion of Cézanne in the brushwork. *The Picnic* (p. 12) of 1924 is an ambitious work, carefully composed and owing a good deal to the inspiration of Gauguin and Picasso.

In *The Musician* of 1925 and *The Return* of 1927 (p. 13) one can detect for the first time the emergence of a distinct artistic personality. The strong emphasis on diagonals in both compositions, the large sweeping rhythms, the easy command of forms in space, the expressionistic distortions or exaggerations of feature or gesture, the humorous mood of one picture and the romantic implications of the other — all these are to become characteristic of Watkins' paintings henceforth.

In 1931, at the age of 37, he was suddenly catapulted into the national limelight when he won first prize at the Carnegie International Exhibition with his *Suicide in Costume* (p. 15). The picture provoked a storm of criticism from the public and from many of the critics. Even those who approved the choice of an unknown young American for this international distinction were moderate in their praise of the painting itself. Conservative critics called it an example of ugly modernism. Some progressives felt it was somewhat derivative. It is difficult to understand today why such a picture created so great a furor. Perhaps in the depths of the depression the public was more repelled than usual by the morbid subject of suicide. However that may be,

6

I think we must now admit that while the painting shows great technical dexterity, the subject is theatrical and the exaggerated pose of the figure appears contrived for purposes of foreshortening and is somewhat unconvincing emotionally.

There is perhaps a similar straining after effect in several small Crucifixions done in 1931 (p. 14). Here, the distortions of the forms, the tortured gestures of all the participants in the scene, echoed in the violent cloud formation in the background, express a morbid mood of almost hysterical proportions that is akin to the melodrama of *Suicide in Costume*. There can be no question that the artist in both these subjects is reacting, however sentimentally, to the despair induced by the depression following the financial crash of 1929. Speaking of these years and in connection with these Crucifixion pictures and *Suicide in Costume*, he has said: "I went through a rather morose period of spiking myself up by getting gloomy. Race and religious questions and 'What a mess things are in and getting worse' were fruitful trains of thought."

Following the notoriety attendant upon the winning of the Carnegie prize, Watkins, shocked by the amount of publicity he had received, retired from public view for three years. In 1934 he had his first one-man exhibition at the Rehn Galleries in New York. This same year he designed sets and costumes for *Transcendence*, a ballet set to music by Liszt, with a plot inspired to some degree by the life of Paganini. During the years 1931 to 1934 he turned to subject matter more in keeping with his normal temperament. Gently poetic in feeling, with occasional humorous or whimsical overtones, such canvases as *Soliloquy* (p. 17), *Negro Spiritual* (p. 18) and *The Fire Eater* (p. 19), painted between 1932 and 1934, set the pattern for much of his later painting. In a recent letter he has explained to me how slight the suggestions were from which many of his picture subjects originated:

"I find," he says, "that it is most difficult to probe to the promptings back of pictures. In a few cases people have asked me 'How come?' shortly after the picture was painted, and the brief time lapse has allowed me to trace back a bit. But what I can pick up is superficial — nothing valid about it — just paraphernalia — the props for the play, so to speak. Not the reason the play was written.

"*The Fire Eater* (p. 19). I was drawing in an evening class. No one knew me. It was peaceful and I remember comfort in finding none of my students about. A small group behind me started whispering during the pose. They were abuzz about a sight they'd seen on their way to class — a fire eater. Intrigued away from my drawing, I listened in. At the end of the pose I asked exactly where this sight might be seen. I started painting the thing the next morning, and went on with it, planning always to see the real thing and find help. But I never got around to seeing it. I think I was afraid to: the flame interested me, and the flame within (eaten) somehow seemed to suggest, if I remember correctly, a continuous movement through the core of

7

the figure. And then I believe I sort of thought of something difficult, perhaps painful, being done with the people who stood about gawking — kidding — indifferent.

"*Death in the Orchard* (p. 32). I was driving on a cement highway on a hot summer day. I passed an animal that had been run over. Its body had been flattened again and again and sun-baked for hours. Nothing left but a little fur and parchment. Too bad, I thought, this waste on cement. The poor field at the roadside could have used the nourishment of the carcass. This event and mind-wandering preceded *Death in the Orchard*. I want sometime to try and do better wings fluttering down through branches.

"*Solitaire* (p. 16). Just men mooning around about themselves (palm reading, fortune telling perhaps). Cards interested me briefly. *Poison for the King* was from a playing card. Maybe someone trumped my King.

"*Negro Spiritual* (p. 18). I heard a fine Negro choir at the Barnes Foundation sing 'Dis ain't the Preacher but it's me, O Lord.' It echoed in my head and the picture was the result. *Springtime* (p. 20) had something to do with an old model I used. I got more out of her thinking about her later than working from her. She had some kind of nervous regret that went into her bones. I didn't actually use her for the picture."

Aside from such subject pictures, a few still lifes (pp. 12, 27) and a rare landscape, *Autumn Recollections*, Watkins has produced from time to time some of the finest portraits painted today in America. This can be said, I think, without qualification. Most modern painters have avoided the commissioned portrait because they refused to be bound by conventional portrait requirements of a good likeness or a flattering pose. Watkins, without sacrificing his independence of expression or giving in to conventions, has succeeded in dignifying his sitters by going beyond mere likeness and studio pose and painting a picture first of all. His sensitive perception of personality, often conveyed through a casual gesture, and by relating the sitter to his own intimate surroundings (pp. 21, 24 and 26), is the most outstanding feature of his work. And even in a more traditional vein, and probably owing some of its solidity and force to Eakins' example, his monumental *Justice Owen J. Roberts* (p. 30) is a vital and authoritative characterization in contrast to the insipid emptiness of most official portraits. On occasion, also, he has painted one or two genre portraits which are related in imaginative temper and in their whimsical air of reverie to a number of his subject pieces. *Fanciful Meeting Long Ago* (p. 29), for example, was painted, I believe, from daguerreotypes of the two children, and *Remember Me* (p. 31) is a souvenir portrait of an English girl who lived for a time with an American family during the last war.

In recent years Watkins has returned to paintings of a religious nature and in fact has produced in this category his major pictures to date: the large *Death* and *Resurrection* canvases in the McIlhenny collection (p. 38 and

8

color plate facing p. 38). Previous to this commission he had hopes of getting one from a church, but this project did not materialize. He had painted, without commission, a *Resurrection* in 1943 (p. 33). Mr. McIlhenny had seen and liked it, and with this picture as a point of departure the artist proceeded to work for two and a half years until the final panels were completed in 1948. To fully appreciate their significance from an emotional and compositional standpoint, they should be studied in relation to the first *Resurrection*, the *Death in the Orchard* of 1938, and to the many studies which led up to the final pictures.

The latter make use of a minimum of traditional imagery or symbolism. The *Death* is slightly indebted to traditional depictions of the Entombment and the Women at the Sepulchre. The cross is barely suggested in the dark opening of the tomb to the left. But in the main this is a very personal interpretation of the subject. The sober color harmonies, browns, greens and violets, and the broad elegiac rhythms of the composition tell their own "story" without recourse to obvious symbolic properties. The impressive restraint and simplicity of this conception of death was arrived at only after considerable thought and preparation. This becomes clear if one follows the genesis of the composition step by step. In his first two studies, *Descent No. 1* (p. 35) and *Descent No. 2*, Watkins attempted to convey the idea of death through the traditional representation of the Descent from the Cross. He abandoned this conception, perhaps because he was forced to use too many conventional properties whose significance had insufficient meaning for him. The first suggestion for the final composition is contained in *To the Tomb* (p. 35). This study is developed further in *The Beloved Dead* (p. 36). The latter sketch has a number of traditional features later discarded or considerably altered: the cross prominently displayed behind the mourning women, the architectural tomb to the left, the mourner with a lamp illuminating the shrouded body. In the next study (p. 37, top) the cross has been removed; the tomb has been extended to give a strong horizontal accent to the composition; the pose of the angel holding the lamp has been changed; and the mourners formerly around the cross have been grouped to the extreme right. The final study (p. 37, bottom) contains all the essentials of the finished picture. Here hovering angels have been introduced, recalling those in *Death in the Orchard* and the 1943 *Resurrection*, but where, in the earlier pictures, their flight is precipitate, in *Death*, their progress is reduced to a slow, horizontal motion, the long rhythms of their movements more in keeping with the funereal subject. The sepulchre has given place to a rock-like tomb, and two powerful vertical columns now divide the composition triptych-wise. In the finished canvas he places these dividing pillars in different planes thus giving a greater depth to the composition.

Watkins tells me that, despite the changes indicated in these various studies, the *Death* canvas was completed fairly quickly. The *Resurrection* occupied him for a much longer time, partly, he says, because the subject gave him more enjoyment. In contrast to the *Death*, however, the *Resurrection* took almost final shape from the beginning (p. 40, top). The motif of the three angels before a curtain, behind which rise the flames symbolizing rebirth, is obviously derived from a similar arrangement in the 1943 *Resurrection*. In later studies (pp. 40 and 41) these angels undergo several slight changes and one important rearrangement. The angel holding the left-hand corner of the curtain receives several changes of costume, first a hoop-skirted garment, then a toga-like cloak and lastly a Martian-like jerkin. The angel to right of center who first carries a key is deprived of this symbol of life in all further studies and is ultimately given another resurrection symbol, a budding branch. And finally the third angel to the right is raised up into the branches of a tree, a device reminiscent of figures in a mediaeval Tree of Life. The crown of thorns in the foreground, one of the more obvious traditional symbols, is in the end linked with the lance, another instrument of Christ's Passion. In three studies of angels Watkins toyed with the idea of giving them more individualized features (p. 39, right) but, he has told me, the result tended to emphasize the importance of the angels too much and to detract from the overall mood of buoyancy and life he wished to convey. In one study the central angel is shown standing before a grove of trees (p. 39, left), but in the final picture the trees are moved to the right and the angel returns to his former position before the curtain.

Returning to the finished pictures, I think what impresses one most about them is not merely their great size (9′ x 14′ 4″), but the dignity and simplicity of their conception. That such convincing directness of emotional expression has been achieved by a very subtle balance of forms and rhythms in the compositions and by a most sensitive series of color harmonies, without any obvious parade of technical virtuosity, is a mark of Watkins' character as an artist and his sincerity and honesty as a man.

A.C.R.

Paul P. Cret. 1922. Oil on canvas, 17½ x 21½". Collection Mrs. Paul P. Cret, Philadelphia, Pa.

The Picnic. c. 1924. Oil on canvas, 74 x 40″. Collection
Mr. and Mrs. R. Sturgis Ingersoll, Penllyn, Pa.

Right: *Still Life.* 1923. Oil on canvas, 26 x 20″. Collection
Mrs. Morris Wenger, Philadelphia, Pa.

The Return. 1927. Oil on canvas, 30½ x 35½". Collection Harry G. Sundheim, Philadelphia, Pa.

Musician. 1925. Oil on canvas, 60 x 36". Frank K. M. Rehn Galleries, New York

Crucifixion. 1931. Oil on canvas, 28 x 22″. Collection Harry G. Sundheim, Philadelphia, Pa.

Suicide in Costume. 1931. Oil, tempera and pastel on canvas, 33¼ x 41¼". Philadelphia Museum of Art, Philadelphia, Pa.

15

Solitaire. 1937. Oil on canvas, 27 x 30¾″. Smith College Museum of Art, Northampton, Mass.

16

Soliloquy. 1932. Oil on canvas, 25 x 30". The Whitney Museum of American Art, New York

Negro Spiritual. c. 1932. Oil on canvas, 54 x 36″. Randolph-Macon Woman's College,
Lynchburg, Va.

The Fire Eater. 1933-34. Oil on canvas, 60¾ x 39″. Philadelphia Museum of Art, Philadelphia, Pa.

Springtime. 1936. Oil on canvas, 54¾ x 35⅝". Santa Barbara Museum of Art, Santa Barbara, Calif.

R. Sturgis Ingersoll. 1938. Oil on canvas, 23 x 24″. Collection Mr. and Mrs. R. Sturgis Ingersoll, Penllyn, Pa.

The Studio. 1940. Oil on canvas, 26 x 30¼″. Albright Art Gallery, Buffalo, N.Y. Room of Contemporary Art

Boris Blai. 1938. Oil on canvas, 40 x 35". The Museum of Modern Art, gift of A. Conger Goodyear

Above: *Thomas Raeburn White*. 1940.
Oil on canvas, 34½ x 45″. Collection
Mr. and Mrs. Thomas Raeburn White,
Philadelphia, Pa.

Mrs. C. E. Etnier. c. 1941. Oil on canvas, 21¾ x 20⅜″. Collection Stephen
Etnier, South Harpswell, Me.

J. Stogdell Stokes. 1943. Oil on canvas, 35 x 27″. Philadelphia Museum of Art, Philadelphia, Pa.

Henry P. McIlhenny. 1941. Oil on canvas, 47 x 33". Collection Henry P. McIlhenny, Philadelphia, Pa.

26

Above: *Miss Rosemary Thompson*. 1941. Oil on canvas,
31 x 32". Collection Mr. and Mrs. Randall Thompson,
Cambridge, Mass.

The Blue Chair. 1941. Oil on canvas, 34 x 25". William
Rockhill Nelson Gallery of Art, Kansas City, Mo.

Mrs. John F. Steinman. 1943. Oil on canvas, 39 x 35½". Collection Mr. and Mrs. John F. Steinman, Lancaster, Pa.

Fanciful Meeting Long Ago. 1945. Oil on canvas, 31 x 45½". Collection Mrs. Herbert C. Morris, Mount Airy, Pa.

Justice Owen J. Roberts. 1947. Oil on canvas, 50 x 40″. The Law School, University of Pennsylvania, Philadelphia, Pa.

Remember Me. 1945. Oil on canvas, 49¼ x 32¼". Collection Mr. and Mrs. Henry D. Sharpe, Providence, R.I.

Death in the Orchard. 1938. Oil on canvas, 42 x 38″. Collection Mr. and Mrs. John F. Steinman, Lancaster, Pa.

Resurrection. 1943. Oil on canvas, 40 x 41″. International Business Machines Corporation, New York. Permanent Collection, Fine Arts Department

The Angel Will Turn a Page in the Book. 1944. Oil on canvas, 33¼ x 28″. The Phillips Gallery, Washington, D.C.

Descent, No. 1. 1947. Oil and tempera on canvas, 12 x 20″. Private collection

To the Tomb. 1947. Oil and charcoal on gesso panel, 15 x 18″. Frank K. M. Rehn Galleries, New York

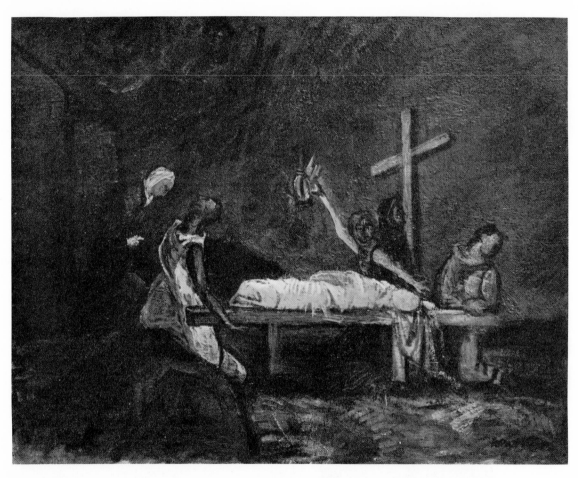

Beloved Dead. 1947. Oil and tempera on canvas, 22 x 28″. Frank K. M. Rehn Galleries, New York

Study for *Death*. 1947. Watercolor, 19 x 32". Collection Henry P. McIlhenny, Philadelphia, Pa.

Study for *Death*. 1947. Oil and tempera on canvas, 40 x 76". Owned by the artist

Death. 1947-48. Oil and egg tempera on canvas, 9′ x 14′ 4″. Collection Henry P. McIlhenny, Philadelphia, Pa.

Color plate: *Resurrection.* 1947-48. Oil and egg tempera on canvas, 9′ x 14′ 4″. Collection Henry P. McIlhenny, Philadelphia, Pa.

Angel Posed. 1947. Oil and charcoal on gesso panel,
18 x 15″. Frank K. M. Rehn Galleries, New York

Right: *Angel.* 1948. Oil on canvas, 76 x 40″. Detroit
Institute of Arts, Detroit, Mich.

Resurrection, No. 1. 1947. Oil on canvas, 18 x 24″. Frank K. M. Rehn Galleries, New York

Resurrection, No. 2. 1947. Oil on canvas, 17 x 28″. Collection Mr. and Mrs. John F. Steinman, Lancaster, Pa.

40

Study for *Resurrection*. 1947. Watercolor, 19 x 33". Collection Henry P. McIlhenny, Philadelphia, Pa.

Study for *Resurrection*. 1947. Oil and tempera on canvas, 40 x 76". Owned by the artist

CHRONOLOGY

1894   Born New York City, December 30. Childhood spent in Rye, N.Y., Louisville, Ky. and Winston Salem, N.C.

1911-12   University of Virginia.

1912-13   University of Pennsylvania.

1913   Entered The Pennsylvania Academy of the Fine Arts.

1914   Left the Academy to work in New York City.

1916   Returned to The Pennsylvania Academy.

1917   Received Cresson Travelling Fellowship — withheld owing to war conditions. Enlisted in Naval Camouflage.

1918   Returned to The Pennsylvania Academy. Received second Cresson Travelling Scholarship.

1918-23   Worked with advertising agency in New York City.

1923   Exercised both travelling scholarships. Travelled for a year in France, Spain and Italy. Studied particularly the work of El Greco, Goya, Piero della Francesca, Andrea del Castagno, Tintoretto and Giorgione.

1926   Returned to Europe for nine months travel; visited Sicily, North Africa and France.

1927   Exhibited with six other Philadelphia painters at the Wildenstein Gallery, New York.

1931   Won first prize at Carnegie International Exhibition, Pittsburgh, with *Suicide in Costume*.

1934   First one-man exhibition at Frank K. M. Rehn Galleries, New York.

1935 to present   Has taught painting at Stella Elkins Tyler School of Fine Arts in Philadelphia and, more recently, at The Pennsylvania Academy of the Fine Arts.

ADVICE TO STUDENTS*

BY FRANKLIN C. WATKINS

The following notes are from comments prompted by particular paintings or drawings examined in the class-room.

If our urges are proper, the sources of our material supply are at hand in our surroundings.

There is surely something inconsistent and superficial in the approach which for variety's sake, poses the model with infinite care to twist the torso, differ each arm and leg, from the other; but then, if it happens to be in full face, paints a repetition on either side of the head's center line. Variety, if it is to be consistent and coincident throughout, comes with the painted thing. Since the variety is in the painting itself and not in the posed object why waste so much ingenuity on the pose? The same must be true with other elements of design. A composition cannot be posed in advance any more than one can find a balanced novel or short story ready-made in a news item.

Don't fake an agility and cleverness to your outline that you don't possess. Let your natural writing form itself. If it trembles and falters it may be your way and time may improve your touch. A writer's character and thought is more legible in engraver's script; but it is separate from it. Your thought and character is in the script itself.

Think of black not as darkness but as a color; black velvet is less black in shadow. Black like other colors lives in light.

Too much light bleaches color, too little fails to reveal.

Some colors seem to have more power than others to expand if surrounded properly by a neutral or breathing zone or a zone in which the insistence of its own color is not too stifling. These zones themselves often add up in the whole picture to an indefinite and indefinable bouquet which we take away with us and recollect as thoughts of lavender or thoughts of blue, or brown, or pink; but, on returning, we cannot find from where it came, nor quite explain the color in our memory.

Equal quantities of complementary colors do not make a maximum contrast — they repeat equal powers.

*Excerpts from a longer text first published in the *Magazine of Art,* December, 1941, under the title, *A Painter Talks to his Students.*

Don't always look directly at the area whose color you are trying to determine. When a color you seek escapes you look away from it, perhaps with unfocused eyes at the surrounding colors, and sometimes in your half-vision, your imagination will supply your color need; and you may see the color in relation to the others.

When certain strong colors break through resistance, as through an overtone, not equally but in climaxes, it seems to give us a feeling of exaltation to a degree that is lacking when they are originally free.

An empty space should be pregnant and full-functioning.

Sculpture students in my school used to refer to painting as a lot of tricks on a flat surface. I used to brood over this; but as time goes on I have been unable to discover a good painter who does not glory in this flatness and those "tricks"; and, in order that his own delight may be shared, he strives that they carry no deception.

Thin color has nothing to do with the consistency of your pigment. It is rather color that does not imply that there is a flat canvas beneath. Acknowledge this flat canvas, this resistance to easy penetration, even when you paint a thin sky. Consciousness of this flat canvas will help your strong colors to sit down and behave.

Don't paint the sky equally deep when you see it through the branches of trees. In some places let the blue appear to come to you, in some places let it suck you in, and it will reach climaxes of intensities, either in itself, or because the colors against it differ from each other and make it appear to change; or it will vary just because you need it to do so. You should control the depths in your whole canvas this way but more broadly.

Art is man's refuge from nature whose confusion is beyond his control, whose order he cannot perceive.

There seems to be in us a natural tendency to rhythm. We incline towards repetitions and accents of a measured pulse.

We seem to look first at people's eyes in life and search them constantly.

Two eyes in a head repeat an already insistent design (spot in circle); vary them — whiter whites in one, darker darks, different high lights, flecks of color. Let one be more intense so that you don't look back and forth, back and forth equally.

43

This applies to other shape repetitions, ears, cheeks, nostrils, etc. If a two-beat gets too much of a start one's imagination may keep it going, seeing it where it does not even exist.

Take care that eyebrows or other accents like curls or pockets in the hair don't steal from the power of the eyes. Eyes usually demand dominance; man has always acknowledged this — made them too large, jewelled them, etc. A closed eye or even a blind eye has an expression — or we see an expression in it.

Avoid a literary solution to the problem of facial expression. Mona Lisa's expression is completely neutral and so becomes all things to all men, for they make of it what they please or can imagine.

A painted head must add up to something. It must arrive at a climax in paint, to a climax in seen detail, and to a general summing up of the character. This involves many departures from the look of the thing. Sometimes in a large composition where there are many heads, and to avoid redundancy, some of the heads may be broken up through shadows, lighting, etc., into small sizes; but in a portrait the head should be complete.

Shapes act powerfully on one another if their intrinsic forms are separated and contrasted, such as the egg form of a head and the squareness of the shoulders. In some characters, underlying shock is important together with little shocks. In other characters harmonizing may be important.

I remember a portrait painter saying to me: "You should try to make your models look as if they were breathing in, not breathing out."

Sometimes a big movement or spin may be created by having forms advance on one side of a head and recede on the other. Hair forward on one side, back on the other; not so far around the collar on one side as on the other, etc. Sculptors sometimes emphasize the convex on one side, the concave on the other.

The manner and degree of a painter's departure from the actual look of things may measure his meaning, and our photograph of objects may act subconsciously as a stepping stone for us into his emotionalities, or as a yardstick; which is sacrificed in extreme abstraction where no resemblance to the actual object is retained.

A man distorts familiar objects with assurance, for he knows his rights. He is uncertain in a strange environment or in a foreign country.

In connection with taking liberties with the look of things: A lithographer in selecting colors for lithographic inks asked Toulouse-Lautrec, "What color should I make the floor?"

Lautrec answered, "Purple or brown."

But when the lithographer asked him what color to make the roast beef, Lautrec answered, "Why roast beef color, of course."

Whether this is a true story or not, it illustrates the point that certain objects will allow greater liberties and more distortion than others. When you stop to think of it, gas light can be green and still be light, but turn roast beef any other color, and what roast beefiness remains? What happens to roast beef through distorting its color may also happen to some things in ill-considered distortion to other forms.

Aerial perspective teaches that colors and objects dim in the distance. If you paint them this way the inducement to recede into the picture and experience the picture's depth becomes too mild. It is necessary, sometimes, to force the experience of depth by accents and powers in the picture's distance and at the same time silence intensities in the foreground.

Checking and re-checking one's own ideas of success may squelch ridicule of a proper failure. I think it was Bette Davis who said: "My idea of a failure is a woman whose idea of success is a mink coat."

In paint, the means cannot justify an end; they are inseparable from it, and little deceptions, little cover-ups, may jeopardize the integrity of the whole. Good painters know it is not easy and they are more lenient than amateurs towards fumbling in the right direction, so don't try too hard to conceal it. Please yourself first, then address yourself to good painters; then just to people; last to amateurs.

It seems to me that only the strong painters can be tender without going sappy, and I doubt those who are continually pointing in their paint to their virility.

Disagreeable sensations may promote impulses as active as agreeable sensations. Should we then leave them to sour in our belly?

Great painters, with all their findings, have always found the wherewithal to seek again.

And a great painting, expanding ever beyond our understanding, induces growth, and growth is life.

Therefore, if a painter says to you, "I know," ask him if he also knows that he is dead on his feet.

44

LENDERS TO THE EXHIBITION

Mr. and Mrs. Leonard T. Beale, Philadelphia, Pennsylvania; Mrs. Paul P. Cret, Philadelphia, Pennsylvania; Stephen Etnier, South Harpswell, Maine; Mrs. Anthony Haswell, Dayton, Ohio; Mr. and Mrs. R. Sturgis Ingersoll, Penllyn, Pennsylvania; International Business Machines Corporation, New York; Mr. and Mrs. Bernard A. Kohn, Philadelphia, Pennsylvania; Mr. and Mrs. William S. Louchheim, Los Angeles, California; Henry P. McIlhenny, Philadelphia, Pennsylvania; Mrs. Herbert C. Morris, Mount Airy, Pennsylvania; Mr. and Mrs. Henry D. Sharpe, Providence, Rhode Island; Mr. and Mrs. Rodolphe Meyer de Schauensee, Devon, Pennsylvania; Mr. and Mrs. John F. Steinman, Lancaster, Pennsylvania; Harry G. Sundheim, Philadelphia, Pennsylvania; Mr. and Mrs. Randall Thompson, Cambridge, Massachusetts; Franklin C. Watkins, Philadelphia, Pennsylvania; Mrs. Morris Wenger, Philadelphia, Pennsylvania; Mr. and Mrs. Thomas Raeburn White, Philadelphia, Pennsylvania.

The Albright Art Gallery, Buffalo, New York; Corcoran Gallery of Art, Washington, D. C.; Detroit Institute of Arts, Detroit, Michigan; The Law School, University of Pennsylvania, Philadelphia, Pennsylvania; The Metropolitan Museum of Art, New York; Newark Museum Association, Newark, New Jersey; Philadelphia Museum of Art, Philadelphia, Pennsylvania; The Phillips Gallery, Washington, D. C.; Randolph-Macon Woman's College, Lynchburg, Virginia; Santa Barbara Museum of Art, Santa Barbara, California; Smith College Museum of Art, Northampton, Massachusetts; The Whitney Museum of American Art, New York; William Rockhill Nelson Gallery of Art, Kansas City, Missouri.

Frank K. M. Rehn Galleries, New York.

CATALOG OF THE EXHIBITION
(March 21 to June 11, 1950)

An asterisk (*) preceding the catalog number indicates that the picture is illustrated. In listing the dimensions, height precedes width.

*1 PAUL P. CRET. 1922. Oil on canvas, 17½ x 21½". Lent by Mrs. Paul P. Cret, Philadelphia, Pa. *Ill. p.* 11

*2 STILL LIFE. 1923. Oil on canvas, 26 x 20". Lent by Mrs. Morris Wenger, Philadelphia, Pa. *Ill. p.* 12

*3 THE PICNIC. c. 1924. Oil on canvas, 74 x 40". Lent by Mr. and Mrs. R. Sturgis Ingersoll, Penllyn, Pa. *Ill. p.* 12

*4 MUSICIAN. 1925. Oil on canvas, 60 x 36". Lent by the Frank K. M. Rehn Galleries, New York. *Ill. p.* 13

*5 THE RETURN. 1927. Oil on canvas, 30½ x 35½". Lent by Harry G. Sundheim, Philadelphia, Pa. *Ill. p.* 13

*6 SUICIDE IN COSTUME. 1931. Oil, tempera and pastel on canvas, 33¼ x 41¼". Lent by the Philadelphia Museum of Art, Philadelphia, Pa. *Ill. p.* 15

*7 CRUCIFIXION. 1931. Oil on canvas, 28 x 22". Lent by Harry G. Sundheim, Philadelphia, Pa. *Ill. p.* 14

*8 NEGRO SPIRITUAL. c. 1932. Oil on canvas, 54 x 36". Lent by Randolph-Macon Woman's College, Lynchburg, Va. *Ill. p.* 18

*9 SOLILOQUY. 1932. Oil on canvas, 25 x 30". Lent by The Whitney Museum of American Art, New York. *Ill. p.* 17

10 OLD WOMAN READING PROOF. c. 1933. Oil on canvas, 40 x 30". Lent by the Newark Museum Association, Newark, N.J.

11 RELIGIOUS EXPERIENCE (design for mural competition for U.S. Customs House, Philadelphia). c. 1933. Oil on panel, 11¼ x 30½". Lent by the Frank K. M. Rehn Galleries, New York.

12 THE ORIGIN OF LANGUAGE (design for mural competition for U.S. Customs House, Philadelphia). c. 1933. Oil on panel, 11¼ x 30½". Lent anonymously

*13 THE FIRE EATER. 1933-34. Oil on canvas, 60¾ x 39". Lent by the Philadelphia Museum of Art, Philadelphia, Pa. *Ill. p.* 19

14 POISON FOR THE KING. 1934. Oil on canvas, 24 x 28". Lent by Harry G. Sundheim, Philadelphia, Pa.

15 BLACK DUCK. 1934. Oil on canvas, 28 x 34". Lent by Mr. and Mrs. William S. Louchheim, Los Angeles, Calif.

16 TRANSCENDENCE: 14 watercolor designs for the ballet produced by the American Ballet Company, 1934. 11 designs for costume, various sizes, 13½ x 9⅜" to 14⅜ x 19⅞"; 3 designs for scenery, 4¼ x 7"; 16 x 24⅞"; 12 x 18⅞". The Museum of Modern Art, acquired through the Lillie P. Bliss Bequest

17 GABRIEL. c. 1935. Oil on canvas, 36 x 40". Lent by the Frank K. M. Rehn Galleries, New York

*18 SPRINGTIME. 1936. Oil on canvas, 54¾ x 35⅜". Lent by the Santa Barbara Museum of Art, Santa Barbara, Calif. *Ill. p.* 20

*19 SOLITAIRE. 1937. Oil on canvas, 27 x 30¾". Lent by the Smith College Museum of Art, Northampton, Mass. *Ill. p.* 16

*20 DEATH IN THE ORCHARD. 1938. Oil on canvas, 42 x 38". Lent by Mr. and Mrs. John F. Steinman, Lancaster, Pa. *Ill. p. 32*

*21 BORIS BLAI. 1938. Oil on canvas, 40 x 35". The Museum of Modern Art, gift of A. Conger Goodyear. *Ill. p. 23*

*22 R. STURGIS INGERSOLL. 1938. Oil on canvas, 23 x 24". Lent by Mr. and Mrs. R. Sturgis Ingersoll, Penllyn, Pa. *Ill. p. 21*

23 SUMMER FRAGRANCE. 1938. Oil on canvas, 39 x 50¾". Lent by the Corcoran Gallery of Art, Washington, D.C.

*24 THE STUDIO. 1940. Oil on canvas, 26 x 30¼". Lent by the Albright Art Gallery, Buffalo, N.Y. Room of Contemporary Art. *Ill. p. 22*

*25 THOMAS RAEBURN WHITE. 1940. Oil on canvas, 34½ x 45". Lent by Mr. and Mrs. Thomas Raeburn White, Philadelphia, Pa. *Ill. p. 24*

26 AUTUMN RECOLLECTIONS. 1940. Oil on canvas, 28 x 31". Lent by The Phillips Gallery, Washington, D.C.

*27 MISS ROSEMARY THOMPSON. 1941. Oil on canvas, 31 x 32". Lent by Mr. and Mrs. Randall Thompson, Cambridge, Mass. *Ill. p. 27*

*28 HENRY P. MC ILHENNY. 1941. Oil on canvas, 47 x 33". Lent by Henry P. McIlhenny, Philadelphia, Pa. *Ill. p. 26*

*29 MISSES MAUDE AND MAXINE MEYER DE SCHAUENSEE. 1941. Oil on canvas, 50 x 40⅛". Lent by Mr. and Mrs. Rodolphe Meyer de Schauensee, Devon, Pa. *Color frontispiece*

*30 MRS. C. E. ETNIER. c. 1941. Oil on canvas, 21¾ x 20⅜". Lent by Stephen Etnier, South Harpswell, Me. *Ill. p. 24*

*31 THE BLUE CHAIR. 1941. Oil on canvas, 34 x 25". Lent by the William Rockhill Nelson Gallery of Art, Kansas City, Mo. *Ill. p. 27*

*32 J. STOGDELL STOKES. 1943. Oil on canvas, 35 x 27". Lent by the Philadelphia Museum of Art, Philadelphia, Pa. *Ill. p. 25*

*33 MRS. JOHN F. STEINMAN. 1943. Oil on canvas, 39 x 35½". Lent by Mr. and Mrs. John F. Steinman, Lancaster, Pa. *Ill. p. 28*

*34 RESURRECTION. 1943. Oil on canvas, 40 x 41". Lent by International Business Machines Corporation, New York. Permanent Collection, Fine Arts Department. *Ill. p. 33*

*35 THE ANGEL WILL TURN A PAGE IN THE BOOK. 1944. Oil on canvas, 33¼ x 28". Lent by The Phillips Gallery, Washington, D.C. *Ill. p. 34*

36 WHITE ROSES. 1945. Oil on canvas, 27 x 37⅛". Lent by The Metropolitan Museum of Art, New York

*37 REMEMBER ME. 1945. Oil on canvas, 49¼ x 32¼". Lent by Mr. and Mrs. Henry D. Sharpe, Providence, R.I. *Ill. p. 31*

*38 FANCIFUL MEETING LONG AGO. 1945. Oil on canvas, 31 x 45½". Lent by Mrs. Herbert C. Morris, Mount Airy, Pa. *Ill. p. 29*

*39 JUSTICE OWEN J. ROBERTS. 1947. Oil on canvas, 50 x 40". Lent by The Law School, University of Pennsylvania, Philadelphia, Pa. *Ill. p. 30*

40 ANTHONY HASWELL. 1948. Oil on canvas, 38¾ x 28¾". Lent by Mrs. Anthony Haswell, Dayton, Ohio

*41 DESCENT, NO. 1. 1947. Oil and tempera on canvas, 12 x 20". Lent anonymously. *Ill. p. 35*

42 DESCENT, NO. 2. 1947. Oil and tempera on canvas, 14 x 14". Lent by Mr. and Mrs. Leonard T. Beale, Philadelphia, Pa.

*43 TO THE TOMB. 1947. Oil and charcoal on gesso panel, 15 x 18". Lent by the Frank K. M. Rehn Galleries, New York. *Ill. p. 35*

*44 BELOVED DEAD. 1947. Oil and tempera on canvas, 22 x 28". Lent by the Frank K. M. Rehn Galleries, New York. *Ill. p. 36*

*45 Study for DEATH. 1947. Watercolor, 19 x 32". Lent by Henry P. McIlhenny, Philadelphia, Pa. *Ill. p. 37*

*46 Study for DEATH. 1947. Oil and tempera on canvas, 40 x 76". Lent by the artist. *Ill. p. 37*

*47 DEATH. 1947-48. Oil and egg tempera on canvas, 9' x 14' 4". Lent by Henry P. McIlhenny, Philadelphia, Pa. *Ill. p. 38*

48 PRAYER. 1947. Oil and tempera on panel, 18 x 15". Lent by Mr. and Mrs. Bernard A. Kohn, Philadelphia, Pa.

49 LAMENT. 1947. Oil on canvas, 30 x 25". Lent by the Frank K. M. Rehn Galleries, New York

50 WINGED FIGURE IN ECSTASY. 1947. Oil and charcoal on gesso panel, 15 x 18". Lent by the Frank K. M. Rehn Galleries, New York

*51 ANGEL POSED. 1947. Oil and charcoal on gesso panel, 18 x 15". Lent by the Frank K. M. Rehn Galleries, New York. *Ill. p. 39*

*52 RESURRECTION, NO. 1. 1947. Oil on canvas, 18 x 24". Lent by the Frank K. M. Rehn Galleries, New York. *Ill. p. 40*

*53 RESURRECTION, NO. 2. 1947. Oil on canvas, 17 x 28". Lent by Mr. and Mrs. John F. Steinman, Lancaster, Pa. *Ill. p. 40*

*54 Study for RESURRECTION. 1947. Watercolor, 19 x 33". Lent by Henry P. McIlhenny, Philadelphia, Pa. *Ill. p. 41*

*55 Study for RESURRECTION. 1947. Oil and tempera on canvas, 40 x 76". Lent by the artist. *Ill. p. 41*

*56 ANGEL. 1948. Oil on canvas, 76 x 40". Lent by the Detroit Institute of Arts, Detroit, Mich. *Ill. p. 39*

*57 RESURRECTION. 1947-48. Oil and egg tempera on canvas, 9' x 14' 4". Lent by Henry P. McIlhenny, Philadelphia, Pa. *Color plate facing p. 38*

46

BIBLIOGRAPHY

This bibliography, with a few exceptions, does not include references to items which have appeared in newspapers. Omitted also are some references to minor exhibition notices, listed in the Art Index 1929-1949.

In the list of exhibition catalogs only those which have been accessible to the compiler are included. They have been arranged chronologically, as have the references to statements by the artist. References to writings on the artist, however, are listed alphabetically under the author's name, or under the title in case of unsigned articles.

All material has been examined by the compiler. Items marked with an asterisk (*) are in the Museum Library.

ANNE BOLLMANN

Abbreviations: Ag August, Ap April, bibl bibliography, col colored, D December, il illustration(s), Ja January, Je June, Mr March, My May, N November, no number(s), O October, p page(s), por portrait, S September.

Sample entry for magazine article: PITZ, HENRY C. Franklin C. Watkins; a painter who walks alone. il(1 col) *American Artist* (New York) 10:20-4 S 1946.

Explanation: An article by Henry C. Pitz, entitled "Franklin C. Watkins; a painter who walks alone" accompanied by illustrations (one of which is in color), will be found in *American Artist* (published in New York), volume 10, pages 20-24, the September 1946 issue.

STATEMENTS BY THE ARTIST

*1 A PAINTER TALKS TO HIS STUDENTS. il *Magazine of Art* (Washington D.C.) 34:504-11 D 1941.
  * Reprinted (with addition of a few paragraphs) under title: "On the teaching of art" in *Painters and sculptors of modern America*; introduction by Monroe Wheeler. p52-60 il New York, Thomas Y. Crowell, 1942.

*2 BENEATH THE PAINT AND VARNISH; technical photographs reveal a strange new world of excitement and wonder. il *Magazine of Art* (Washington D.C.) 37:128-34 Ap 1944.
  Article written by Franklin C. Watkins and Henri Marceau.

*3 EAKINS; PHILADELPHIA'S CENTENARY OF ITS LEADING XIX CENTURY ARTIST: a painter's appreciation of the tradition he once combatted. il *Art News* (New York) 43:10-13 Ap 15 1944.

*4 FOREWORD. In exhibition catalog: RoKo Gallery, New York. *Claude Clark exhibits 26 paintings, April 21-May 11*. folder New York, 1946.

*5 JEAN BAPTISTE CAMILLE COROT. il *Magazine of Art* (Washington D.C.) 39:371-3 D 1946.

*6 THE JURY'S STATEMENT. por *Corcoran Gallery of Art Bulletin* (Washington D.C.) 3no1:3-4 N 1949.
  On the occasion of The Fourth Annual Area Exhibition, addressed "to those whose work was not accepted."
  See also bibl. 23.

BOOKS, ARTICLES, EXHIBITION REVIEWS

7 A[BBOTT], J[ERE]. Other acquisitions. il *Smith College Museum of Art Bulletin* (Northampton, Mass.) no18/19:16-17,18 Je 1938.
  Brief discussion of Watkins and his "Solitaire."

8 BAUM, WALTER EMERSON. Carles and Watkins in retrospect. il *MKR's Art Outlook* (New York) no9:7 Ap 1946.
  Review of exhibition, Philadelphia Museum of Art.

*9 BEAR, DONALD. Watkins paintings, now at museum, are discussed. il *Santa Barbara News Press*, Sunday morning Ag 21 1949.
  Review of exhibition, Santa Barbara Museum of Art.

*10 BRACE, ERNEST. Franklin Watkins. il *American Magazine of Art* (Washington D.C.) 29:723-9 N 1936.

*11 BRAGGIOTTI, GLORIA. Franklin C. Watkins: a painter's painter. il(1 col) *The Studio* (New York & London) 125no600:78-81 Mr 1943.
  BREUNING, MARGARET. See bibl. 14.

*12 CHARLOT, JEAN. Franklin D. (sic) Watkins. il *Hound & Horn* (Camden, N.J.) 7no2:241-3 Ja/Mr 1934.
  * Reprinted in the author's *Art from the Mayans to Disney*. p180-86 il New York, Sheed and Ward, 1939.

*13 CLIFFORD, HENRY. Philadelphia prodigals; Carles and Watkins at the Philadelphia Museum. il *Art News* (New York) 45:40-1,64 Mr 1946.
  ———See also bibl. 37.
  COCHRANE, ALBERT FRANZ. See bibl. 14.

*14 [CRITICISM OF WATKINS' "SUICIDE IN COSTUME"] il *American Magazine of Art* (Washington D.C.) 23:466 D 1933.
  Includes excerpts from criticism by Margaret Breuning, Albert Franz Cochrane, Dorothy Grafly, Edward Alden Jewell.

*15 CRITICS PRONOUNCE WATKINS A ROMANTICIST. il *Art Digest* (New York) 8:9 My 1 1934.
  Review of exhibition, Rehn Galleries, New York. Quoting various other critics.

*16 FOUNDER'S DAY, 1946. THE JURY OF AWARD. por *Carnegie Magazine* (Pittsburgh) 20:107-9 O 1946.
  Watkins, one of three comprising the jury of

award for the Founder's Day Exhibition, Painting in the United States, 1946: p108-9.

*17 F[ROST], R[OSAMUND]. Watkins: much savor, no sugar. *Art News* (New York) 40:27 Ja 15 1942.
Review of exhibition, Rehn Galleries, New York.
GRAFLY, DOROTHY. See bibl. 14.
INGERSOLL, R. STURGIS. See bibl. 37.

*18 INTELLECTUAL ART OF WATKINS DISPLAYED. il *Art Digest* (New York) 16:9 Ja 15 1942.
Review of exhibition, Rehn Galleries, New York.
JEWELL, EDWARD ALDEN. See bibl. 14, 22.
KIRSTEIN, LINCOLN. See bibl. 33.

*19 L[A] F[ARGE], H[ENRY A.]. Spotlight on Watkins. il *Art News* (New York) 47:45 D 1948.
Review of exhibition, Rehn Galleries, New York.

20 LANDGREN, MARCHAL E. Franklin C. Watkins: F.K.M. Rehn gallery: April 16-May 5, 1934. *Trend* (Brooklyn) 2:149-50 My/Je 1934.
Review of exhibition.
McBRIDE, HENRY. See bibl. 33.

*21 O'C[ONNOR], J[OHN]. Portrait [of Owen Josephus Roberts]. il *Carnegie Magazine* (Pittsburgh) 21:98 (il on cover) N 1947.

22 THE PRIZE PICTURE SHOCKS. il *Literary Digest* (New York) 3:16-17 N 7 1931.
Quotes Robert Reiss in *Philadelphia Record* and Edward Alden Jewell in *New York Times*.

*23 PITZ, HENRY C. Franklin C. Watkins; a painter who walks alone. il(1 col) *American Artist* (New York) 10:20-4 S 1946.
Including excerpts from Watkins' classroom criticisms.

*24 REED, JUDITH KAYE. Franklin Watkins portrays life and death. il *Art Digest* (New York) 23:13 D 1 1948.
Review of exhibition, Rehn Galleries, New York.
REISS, ROBERT. See bibl. 22.

*25 SAINT-GAUDENS, HOMER. The American artist and his times. p302,311-13 il New York, Dodd, Mead, 1941.

*26 SCHWARTZ, JANE. Franklin Watkins: Rehn Galleries. *Art News* (New York) 32:9 Ap 21 1934.
Review of exhibition.

*27 WIGHT, FREDERICK S. Milestones of American painting in our century. p114-15 il Boston, Institute of Contemporary Art; New York, Chanticleer Press, 1949.
The book is a "product of an exhibition" at the Institute of Contemporary Art, January 20-March 1, 1949.

*28 WOLF, BEN. Philadelphia honors Carles and Watkins. il *Art Digest* (New York) 20:8,28 Mr 1 1946.
Review of exhibition, Philadelphia Museum.

*29 YOUNG PHILADELPHIAN WINS FIRST PRIZE AT CARNEGIE INTERNATIONAL. il *Art Digest* (New York) 6:3-4 O 15 1931.

EXHIBITION CATALOGS

*30 NEW YORK. MUSEUM OF MODERN ART. Murals by American painters and photographers. p[45] il New York, Museum of Modern Art, 1932.
Biographical note; reproduction of 3 studies and 1 large panel.

*31 REHN, FRANK K.M. GALLERIES, NEW YORK. Paintings by Franklin C. Watkins, April 16 to May 5. folder 1934.
Lists 25 works. Reviewed in bibl. 20,26.

*32 GIMBEL GALLERIES, PHILADELPHIA. Earl Horter: etchings, drawings and aquatints; Franklin Watkins: designs for the ballet "Transcendence." February 6 to February 20. folder 1935.
Lists 13 works by Watkins.

*33 REHN, FRANK K.M. GALLERIES, NEW YORK. Franklin Watkins: designs for ballet "Transcendence," February 26 to March 9. folder 1935.
Lists 13 works. Introduction: "Franklin Watkins and Transcendence" by Lincoln Kirstein. Reviewed by Henry McBride in *The Sun* (New York) Mr 2 1935.

*34 SMITH COLLEGE MUSEUM OF ART, NORTHAMPTON, MASS. 1st New England exhibition: Franklin Watkins. April 11 to April 25. folder [1938].
Lists 22 works. Includes biographical note.

*35 REHN, FRANK K.M. GALLERIES, NEW YORK. Paintings by Franklin C. Watkins; January 5 to January 31. folder 1942.
Lists 18 works plus "a group of drawings for the ballet 'Transcendence.'" Reviewed in bibl. 17,18.

*36 CHICAGO. THE ARTS CLUB. Franklin C. Watkins. Exhibition December 4 to December 26. folder 1942.
Lists 16 works. Includes biographical note.

*37 PHILADELPHIA. MUSEUM OF ART. Paintings by Arthur B. Carles and Franklin C. Watkins. February 17-March 17, 1946. il *Philadelphia Museum Bulletin* 40no208:33-64 Mr 1946.
Lists 33 works by Watkins. Includes prefatory note by Henry Clifford, and foreword by R. Sturgis Ingersoll. Reviewed in bibl. 8,13,28.

*38 REHN, FRANK K.M. GALLERIES, NEW YORK. Paintings on two themes: Franklin C. Watkins. November 15 to December 11. folder 1948.
Lists 14 works: studies for panels on the theme of Crucifixion and Resurrection, made for Henry P. McIlhenny. Reviewed in bibl. 19,24.

*39 SANTA BARBARA. MUSEUM OF ART. Thirty paintings. Exhibition: Stuart Davis, Yasuo Kuniyoshi, Franklin Watkins. July 28 through August 28. 4 leaves il 1949.
Lists 10 works by Watkins. Reviewed in bibl. 9. Exhibition also held at San Francisco, M.H. de Young Memorial Museum, September 8 to October 9, and at Portland, Oregon, Art Museum, October 15 to November 20, with same catalog.